Joseph Fisher

The History of Landholding in Ireland

Joseph Fisher

The History of Landholding in Ireland

ISBN/EAN: 9783337322717

Printed in Europe, USA, Canada, Australia, Japan

Cover: Foto ©ninafisch / pixelio.de

More available books at **www.hansebooks.com**

LANDHOLDING IN

BY

JOSEPH FISHER

FELLOW OF THE ROYAL ...

Author of "The History of Land..."

CO.

INTRODUCTION.

THIS work is an expansion of a paper read at the meeting of the Royal Historical Society in May, 1876. It is published separately to bring it within the reach of those who are not members of that Society, and do not receive the annual volume of its transactions.

The author has been compelled to omit much which he thought pertinent to the subject in order to bring the work within the prescribed limits.

WATERFORD,
December, 1876.

THE HISTORY

OF

LANDHOLDING IN IRELAND.

In the paper which I read last year upon the History of Landholding in England, I described the principles which underlie the distribution of land among the aboriginal inhabitants, the primal occupiers of the soil. It is not necessary that I should now dwell at much length upon that portion of the subject. I would, however, refer to two authorities which have weight in relation to the allotment of lands.

Sir William Blackstone says, vol. ii., p. 3,—

"By the law of nature and reason he who first began to use the land, acquired therein a kind of transient possession, that lasted as long as he was using it and no longer; or to speak with greater precision, the *right* of possession continued for the same time as the *act* of possession lasted. But there is no foundation in nature or natural law why a set of words upon parchment should convey the dominion of land; why a son should have a right to exclude his fellow-creatures from a determinate spot of ground because his father had done so before him."

A more recent writer, Kenelm E. Digby ("History of the Law of Real Property," p. 3), says,—

"However its origin is to be accounted for, this idea as to property in land is nearly universal in primitive communities. The land is regarded as the property of the community at large, and individuals as a general rule have only temporary rights of possession or enjoyment upon the lands of the community. The land is public land—*ager publicus*,—folc-land, or land of the people. Dealing with folc-land is the most important of the functions of the chief of the community in time of peace. In dealing with it he always acts, not as supreme landowner, but as the head of the community, in conjunction with the leaders of the second rank."

My inquiries—I can hardly call them studies—led me some years ago to attempt a sketch of the changes in the system of landholding in the various countries of Europe; since then abler minds have worked in the same field. As I pursued my inquiries I thought the systems fell into groups, and that the similarity was mainly owing to *race;* identical institutions are traceable among kindred races. The necessities of humanity were similarly expressed. Land is the sustainer of life. In the language of the "Senchus Mor" it is "perpetual man." Hence arose the need of appropriating a portion to every man, who would otherwise owe his life to him who possessed the land and supplied him with food.

Time is a solvent; the increase of population, the division of labour, the growth of exchange of products, led to some changes. The necessities of conquest set aside primeval ideas. The stronger lived upon the labour of the weaker. Invaders carried their customs with them, and aboriginal systems were submerged in the deluge. The same usage will sometimes be found in two or more countries, but if the matter is followed up it will be found to proceed from the same cause. The *metayer* system of parts of France and Italy is clearly traceable to the inroads of the Burgundians; they formed two armies, one of which settled in France, the other in Italy, and under the name of *Hospitalities*, or payments from the farming occupants of the conquered lands, exacted a stated annual portion of the produce of the land; hence the word *metayer*, to measure.

My inquiries led me to group the land systems; there are the *Celtic*, the *Gothic*, (some prefer using the term *Teutonic*, but the Teutons were not one of the ancient races), the *Scandinavian*, the *Sclavonian*, the *Mongolian* or *Scythic*, and those of the peninsulas, Turkey, Spain, and Italy, which have been more frequently overrun than the northern parts of Europe, and to whose inhabitants older historians apply the term *Scythic*, but the residents on the shores of the Mediterranean should not be confounded with the Scythians of Northern Asia.

The diffusion of men consequent upon the confusion of

tongues led the sons of Japheth* to settle in Europe, while those of Shem and Ham took Asia and Africa. The seven sons of Japheth were *Gomer*, from whom the Celts are descended; *Magog*, the Mongols or Scythians; *Madai*, the Sclavs; *Tubal*, the Goths; *Tiras*, the Scandinavians; *Javan* and *Meshech*, the inhabitants of the isles of Greece, Turkey, Italy, and Spain,† who were called Scythians, but must not be confounded with the Mongols, or Magode, who are traced by Josephus to Magog.

Some recent writers overlook the most ancient and trustworthy of histories, and prefer the writings of Herodotus or Strabo to those of Moses. The latter are, in my opinion, more authentic, they tell us that the descendants of Noah peopled the whole earth. The new theory of development, which is pushed very far, not only with regard to the origin of the human race, but to the origin of institutions,

---

* Gen. x. 2—5: "The sons of Japheth; Gomer, and Magog, and Madai, and Javan, and Tubal, and Meshech, and Tiras. And the sons of Gomer; Ashkenaz, and Riphath, and Togarmah. And the sons of Javan; Elishah, and Tarshish, Kittim, and Dodanim. By these were the isles of the Gentiles divided in their lands; every one after his tongue, after their families, in their nations."

† The Israelites and the Jews continued to apply to the races inhabiting the shores of the Mediterranean the names of their ancestors. Thus Isaiah, chap. xxiii., in predicting the fall of Tyre, says, "Howl, ye ships of *Tarshish;* for it is laid waste, so that there is no house, no entering in from the land of *Chittim*." And again, chap. lxvi. 19, "I will send those that escape unto the nations, to *Tarshish*, Pul, and Lud, that draw the bow, to *Tubal*, and *Javan*, to the isles afar off." This was written about 1,700 years after the deluge, but it shows that the Jews of that day preserved the nomenclature of a bygone age, and attributed the settlement of the Mediterranean to the sons of Japheth, three of whom are stated by name in the latter passage. Ezekiel, speaking of Tyre (chap. xxvii.), writes, "*Tarshish* was thy merchant by reason of the multitude of all kinds of riches; with silver, iron, tin, and lead, they traded in thy fairs. *Javan*, *Tubal*, and *Meshech*, they were thy merchants: they traded the persons of men and vessels of brass in thy market. They of the house of *Togarmah* traded in thy fairs with horses and horsemen and mules. The men of Dedan [*Dodanim*] were thy merchants; many isles were the merchandise of thine hand."

traces man to the monkey; those who advocate this theory have never shown when the power of developing monkeys into men, if it ever existed, ceased. If it existed it would continue; and unless they can produce a man-monkey, or a monkey-man, they fail to prove that a monkey ever developed into a man, and leave the Biblical narrative intact.

Language and institutions have followed the path of conquest. Mr. Latham, one of the most painstaking writers of philology, asks (" Elements of Philology," p. 611),—

"Has the Sanskrit reached India from Europe, or have the Lithuanic, the Slavonic, the Latin, the Greek, and the German, reached Europe from India? If historical evidence be wanting, the *à priori* presumption must be considered. I submit history is silent, and that the presumptions are in favour of the smaller class having been deduced from the area of the larger, rather than *vice versa*. If so, the *situs* of the Sanskrit is on the eastern or south-eastern frontier of the Lithuanic, and its origin is European." He adds, " A mile is a mile, and a league a league, from whatever end it is measured; and it is no further from the Danube to the Indus than from the Indus to the Danube. . . . The fact of a language being not only projected, so to say, to another region, but entirely lost in its own, is anything but unique. There is no English in Germany. A better example, however, is found in the Magyar of Hungary, of which no trace is to be found within some 700 miles of its present area. Yet the Magyar is not twelve hundred years old in Europe."

The absence of English from Germany is quite in harmony with my assertions that the Anglo-Saxons were Scandinavian, and that there was a complete migration of the Jutes, the Angles, and the Saxons, from the north of the Elbe into England, in the fifth and sixth centuries.

Looking at settlements from a philological point of view, it appears that the use of duplicate words is evidence of conquest; that such words as omnipotent, almighty, omniscient, all-seeing, ox, beef, sheep, mutton, bear the impress of two races, the conqueror and the conquered. Institutions bear the same imprint, though it is more difficult to separate their component parts than it is to follow the stream of language; but if we could follow back the branch to the trunk, we should arrive at the point of separation, which is also the point of union.

Herodotus gives the Celts the large domains of Central Europe north of the Danube, extending from the Black Sea to the ocean. There has been a westward movement of ancient races; the Mongols have possessed themselves of parts of the land of the Scandinavians and the Sclavs, the Scandinavians of some of those of the Celts, the Sclavs have taken those of the Goths, the Goths have swarmed over into Celtic possessions, and also into the peninsulas of Italy and Spain; while the Turks, the only Asiatic rulers in Europe, have held for several centuries part of the domains of the Southern Scythians. I have depicted upon maps of Europe the location of these races, in ancient and in the present time, and may perhaps publish them and the result of my researches at some future time.

My present task is to deal with that portion of the Celtic race which settled in Ireland, and where, being out of the high road of invasion, the ancient institutions remained uneffaced long after they had disappeared elsewhere. The general characteristic of the Celts was an unwarlike disposition; being the original occupiers of fertile regions, they spread westward, yet found nothing to war with, hence there was an absence of any domineering or defensive organization. Their institutions appear to have been expressed in the cry of Celtic France at the end of the eighteenth century, "Equality, Liberty, Fraternity." The descendants of Gomer, the parent of the Celts, broke up into separate families, each governed by a patriarch; disintegration was followed by integration, the family grew into the clan, sept, or tribe which was the joint owner of the land occupied by the progenitor, with a life possession to each of his descendants. There was a distinct limitation of the lands to the whole of his descendants, not to one portion to the detriment of others, each generation had the power of apportionment for life, and hence a dissimilarity in the size of the possessions. The lands belonged to the Commune, the primal owners, but were apportioned to the individuals composing the Commune, according to their age and worthiness. This arrangement relates, however, solely to *land* which was created for the use of man, and did not affect *chattels*, which being the products of each man's industry, or the result of his self-denial, were his property and at his own disposal.

The necessity of combined action for defensive purposes led to the union of tribes under a common chief, but each preserved its own leader and usages, and hence arose what is called "Customary laws." These were at various times collected and written down, and form the basis of the *Brehon* code, from the Brehons or judges who were instructed in and administered it. The land system is called *Tanistry*, from the Tanist, an officer elected to succeed the chieftain, whose main office was to divide the land of the tribe among the living members thereof; he was, in fact, a trustee and heir to the land of each of the sept or clan, and made such a division as suited the circumstances of the case. I shall hereafter describe that process in detail.

Ireland appears to have become known to the Greeks about 200 years B.C.; they gave it the title of "Juveonei;" Cæsar calls it "Hibernia," and says it was about half the size of England. Ptolemy gives a map of Ireland, which is superior in accuracy to that of Scotland. The Belgæ had colonized the eastern coasts of England about two centuries before Cæsar's invasion. It is supposed that they settled in Ireland, where they were called Firbolgs; the Romans called them *Scuti*, and the land Scota, by which name it was known in Europe until the twelfth century.

Hume, who evidently considered the Gauls and Irish were Celts, writes (Essay xi. vol. ii. p. 463),—

"We are informed by Cæsar that the Gauls had no fixed property in land, but that the chieftains, when any death happened in a family, made a new division of all the land among the several members of the family. This is the custom of *tanistry* which so long prevailed in Ireland."

Tacitus, who wrote A.D. 78, says of Ireland,—

"The soil and climate, and the disposition and habits of the people, differ not much from Britain; the approaches to the country and its ports are better known through the commercial intercourse of merchantmen."

This implies a state greatly in advance of that which prevailed either in Gaul or Britain.

The Psalter of Cashel asserts that Milesius, who had thirty-two sons, of whom eight arrived in Ireland, landed in that country 1,300 years before the birth of Christ. Amongst the successors of the sons of Milesius, were Heber-Heremon and Ish, and Gadelas, from Gawth Del, a lover of learning; of these kings it is said,—

> "A hundred and ninety-seven years complete
> The Tuatha ad Danaus, a famous colony
> The Irish sceptre swayed."

The most celebrated of these monarchs was Ollamb Fodhla, who reigned A.M. 3082. Keating, the historian, says,—

"He summoned his principal nobility, his Druids, the poets, and historiographers to meet him in a full assembly at Tara once in every three years, to revise the body of the established laws, and to change or correct them as the exigence of affairs required; in testimony of this I shall produce the following verses of great antiquity, and to be found in writings of good authority:—

> "The learned Ollamb Fodhla first ordained
> The great *assembly* where nobles met,
> And priests, and poets, and philosophers,
> To make new laws and to correct the old,
> And to advance the honour of the country.'"

Plowden ("Historical Review of Ireland," p. 15) thus describes the assemblage of the Irish chieftains in the reign of Ollamb Fodlah:—

"Under him was instituted the great Fes at Tramor or Tarah, which was, in fact, a triennial convention of the States or Parliament, the members of which consisted of Druids and other learned men who represented the people in that assembly. Thus the monarch and the provincial and other kings who had the executive power in their hands on one side, and the philosophers and priests, together with the deputies of the people on the other, formed the whole of the ancient legislature. They particularly devoted themselves to the examination and settlement of the historical antiquities and annals of the kingdom; they were rehearsed and privately inspected by a select committee of the most learned members. When they had passed the approbation of the assembly they were transcribed into the authentic chronicle of the nation, which was called the register or *Psalter of Tarah.*"

The seats of the members of the great council were indicated by hanging their coats of arms on the wall over them, thus evincing a complete knowledge of heraldry.

The Brehon Code dates as far back as the reign of Ollamb Fodhla, 850 B.C., and existed unbroken until the invasion of Henry II., 1171 A.D., a period of over two thousand years. It continued to be the law of that portion of Ireland not under English rule until 1603, when it was abolished by resolutions of the Irish judges. Ollamb Fodhla was a contemporary of Hezekiah king of Judah. The codification of the Irish laws took place before the Median kingdom arose, before the Grecian republics were formed, before Rome was founded. Being based upon principles of natural justice, and suited to the requirements of humanity, they survived the fall of these greater states, and were displaced to make room for a system which does not possess the same advantages, but gives the control of the land to a small class, and leaves the mass of the people to struggle for its possession.

The history of landholding in Ireland possesses an additional attraction, it throws light upon the earlier institutions of the Celtic race. The Irish were not an unmixed race. The pre-Christian period of Irish history is marked with traces of an invasion from the Mediterranean, most probably of a Semitic character, and the post-Christian period has distinct traces of evangelization direct from Syria. Those problems in stone, the Irish round towers, which have excited the curiosity and study of so many learned men, without affording a tangible solution, have always appeared to me to be of Semitic origin. The poetic remains of Irish history point to an invasion of Ireland from Egypt, on the expulsion of the dynasty when "a king arose who knew not Joseph." The milder climate of the East permitted the unroofed combustion of the sacred fires, which in the humid climate of Ireland required some covering; the round towers, from their elevation, would display the sacred gleams to large districts. The introduction of Christianity naturally led to the erection of the church in proximity to the round tower, and in some cases to its use as a belfry. The abrasions from the friction of a rope or chain on some of the window-sills prove that there was a rude adaptation of an existing edifice to more modern requirements.

The land system of the earlier Irish race is described by the term TANISTRY. It is derived from the office of the *Tanist*, whose duty was to divide the land of the sept or tribe among the members. The tribe selected the tanist, who succeeded to the chiefry upon the death of the chief. I shall have to refer to his mode of election and duties further on, but it may be convenient to divide the subject into the following:—

1st. The Tanistry, or Communal.
2nd. The Scandinavian, or Mixed.
3rd. The Norman, or Feudal.
4th. The Stuart, or Confiscation.
5th. The Hanoverian, or Unsettled.
6th. The Present.

PART I.—THE TANISTRY OR COMMUNAL PERIOD.

The term *tanistry* was applied to a system of landholding in which the land belonged to the commune while possession was given to the individual. It took its name from the *Tanist*, who was next in point of rank and influence to the chieftain, and succeeded to the vacant chiefry. He was elected by the sept or lineage, and was the distributor of itslands. The *Tanistry* system, though *communal*, inasmuch as no man held the land in severalty, differed in many respects from the village communities of Russia and India. It approached very nearly to that of New Zealand. The ancient Irish law tracts, to which I shall hereafter call your attention, neither enact nor describe it. The system appears to have been antecedent to any written law, and to have been recognised as an existing institution in the same way that customs in England prove common law rights which rest upon the *lex non scripta*.

The descriptions which we possess of this system are comparatively modern, and they are written by strangers, Edmund Spenser in the reign of Queen Elizabeth, and Sir John Davis in that of James I. The latter filled the office of attorney-general, and both looked upon the Irish Tanistry system as uncouth and barbarous.

The customs of the Irish people, as described by Spenser and Davis, must have been more or less tinged by the intermixture of Scandinavian, Norman, or feudal ideas, from contact with the Easterlings, the Danes, and the Anglo-Norman invaders, who had partly occupied or ruled the country for several hundred years before Spenser. Yet their inherent vitality, and thorough adaptation to the wants of humanity, preserved them intact. The author of " The Faerie Queen " was an Irish landholder, resident on the borders of the counties Cork and Waterford. In his " View of Ireland," he thus describes the system of *tanistry* which existed at that time :—

" There be many wide counties in Ireland which the laws of England were never established in, nor any acknowledgment of subjection made, and also even those which are subdued and seem to acknowledge subjection, yet the same Brehon law is practised amongst themselves by reason that dwelling as they do, whole nations and septs of the Irish together, without any Englishman among them, the Irish say that their ancestors had no estate in any lands, seignories, or hereditaments, longer than during their own lives, as they allege, for all the Irish do hold their land by *tanistry*, which is (say they) no more but personal estate for his lifetime, that is *tanist*, by reason that he is admitted thereunto by election of the country.

" It is a custom among all the Irish that presently after the death of any of their chief lords or captains they do presently assemble themselves to a place generally appointed and known unto them, to choose another in his stead, when they do nominate and elect for the most part not the eldest son, nor any of the children of the lord deceased, but the next to him of blood that is the eldest and worthiest, as commonly the next brother unto him if he have any, or the next cousin, or so forth, as any elder in that kindred or sept, and then next to him do they choose the next of the blood to be *tanist*, who shall next succeed him in the said captaincy if he live thereunto.

"They use to place him that shall be their chieftain upon a stone always reserved for that purpose, and placed commonly upon a hill, in some of which I have seen formed and engraven a foot, which they say is the measure of their first captain's foot, wherein he standing receives an oath to preserve all the ancient former customs inviolable, and to deliver up the succession peaceably to his *tanist*, and then hath a wand delivered unto him by some whose proper office that is; after which descending from the stone he turneth himself round, thrice forward and thrice backward.

"For when their captain dieth, if the seignory should descend to his child, and he perhaps an infant, another might peradventure step in between and thrust him out with a strong hand. The *tanist* is always ready known, if it should happen the captain suddenly to die, or to be slain in battle, or to be out of the country to defend and keep it from all doubts and dangers. For which cause the *tanist* hath also a share of the country allotted to him, and certain cuttings and spendings upon all the inhabitants under the lord."

It is well to bear in mind that this description of the inauguration of the tanist, the object of his appointment, and the duties he was expected to perform, is from the pen of an Englishman, and written in the latter portion of the sixteenth century, after an interval of several hundred years from the landing of Henry II., which event followed three centuries of struggle against the Danes and Easterlings.

A few years later, in the early part of the seventeenth century, Sir John Davis, also an Englishman, who occupied the position of attorney-general to James I., and who looked on the existing system as a lawyer, wrote thus ("Reports," p. 134):—

"First, it is to be known that the land possessed by the mere Irish were divided into several territories or counties, and the inhabitants of every Irish county were divided into septs or lineages.

Second, in every Irish territory there was a lord or chieftain, and a *tanist*, who was his successor apparent; and of every Irish sept or lineage there was also a chief, who was called Cean Finny (Cean Fini). Third, all possession within these Irish territories ran always in the course of *tanistry*, or in course of *gavelkind*. Every seignory or chiefry, with the portion of land which passed with it, went without partition to the *tanist*, who always came in by election or strong hand, and not by descent; but all the inferior tenancies were partible between the males in gavelkind. Yet the estate the lord had in chiefry, or the inferior tenants had in gavelkind, was not an estate of inheritance, but of temporary or transitory possession. For as the next heir to the lord or chieftain was not to inherit the chiefry, but the eldest and worthiest of the sept, who was often removed or expelled by another who was more active and strong than he, so the lands of the nature of gavelkind were not partible among the next heirs male of him who died seised, but among the sept in this manner:—The Caen finny or chief of a sept (who was commonly the most ancient of the sept), made all the partitions at his discretion; and after the death of any ter-tenant, who had a competent portion of land, assembled the sept, and having thrown all their possessions into hotchpot, made a new partition of all, in which partition he did not assign to the son of him who died the portion his father had, but he allotted to each of the sept according to his seniority the better or greater portion; these portions or purparties being so allotted or assigned were possessed and enjoyed accordingly until a new partition was made, which at the discretion or will of the Cean finny was to be made on the death of each inferior tenant."

The great difference between *gavelkind* and *tanistry*[*] lay in this,—the former, *gavelkind*, divided a man's land between his sons, each of whom thereby acquired as large an estate in his separate portion as his father had, and on his death it was again divided between the sons of each of them, it being essentially a division *per stirpes*. The latter, *tanistry*, did not give a man's land to his sons, it reverted to the sept, and each of the sons got a portion of the lands of the sept, but it was only a life enjoyment. Under *gavelkind* there was ownership in severalty, which did not exist under *tanistry*.

  [*] The proper term would be *Gableach cime*.

The *tanistry* system seems to have been based upon the idea expressed in Sir John Davis's description, *lineage;* the land had been the possession of some remote ancestor and all his *lineage* were provided for out of it. The *Cean finny* and *Tanist* appear to have held the same office, and its main function was the equitable division of the land among the lineage of the far-away original chieftain. It may sound trite to say that even now every man has only a life possession or life estate, for all love to think that they can exercise a sort of ownership over their lands after death has put them out of possession. This right had no place in the tanistry system, a man enjoyed the land allotted to him while he lived, but when he died the living dealt with it as they deemed best for their own interests.

But this system went further. "Land was to them perpetual man," the staple of existence—therefore every one of the lineage possessed his share for life. The lands of the chief did not descend to his children, they with his office went to the tanist, the lands of the tanist to his successor. All the other lands of the sept were divided among the members; there was no tenancy in the sense in which we use the word; there was no rent, no eviction, none of the powers claimed under the feudal system by the tenants in fee.

This system of *tanistry* was essentially republican in its character, the land vested in the people, not in the Crown; its division was arranged by the elected officer of the sept or lineage; all its members were joint owners of the common estate, which was strictly settled in tail to the whole of the lineage. No man could sell the inheritance of his children, and there were neither landlords nor tenants. The two administrative officers, the chief and the tanist, had their own official demesnes, which did not descend to their children, but went like church land, or clerical income, to him who succeeded to the office.

A system so unique differs in many respects from that of any of the more ancient semi-civilized nations. The Egyptians appear to have owned their land in severalty, for they sold it to Joseph for Pharaoh. The Israelites, though prevented from selling their land in perpetuity, could mortgage it until the year of jubilee, but the tribal lands could not leave the tribe, they descended to the children or next of kin. The Greeks and Romans both recognised ownership in severalty. The *tanistry* system, which reached back to a period more remote than the foundation of Rome, appears to have arisen simultaneously over the entire island, and to have existed, notwithstanding many isolated invasions, until it was partially displaced by the landing of the Anglo-Normans, and was wholly abrogated, not by legislation, but by a legal decision in the reign of James I.

Professor Sullivan's introduction to O'Curry's Essays describes the division of the Irish people into classes. I have endeavoured to condense his statement thus:—In Ireland, as in every other part of Europe, we can trace the existence of the two great classes, the free and the unfree. Amongst the free there were privileged classes called *Aires*: there were two classes of *Aires*, those who possessed land, or *Deis*, who were called *Flaths*, and those who possessed cows or other cattle, who were called *Bo Aires*. The class of tribesmen called *Ceiles* were divided into two categories, the *Saer* or free Ceiles, and the *Daer* or base Ceiles; an ancient manuscript, H. 3, 18, T.C.D., p. 119, says, "It is competent for a man never to accept base wages from any man unless it be his own will to do so, and it is competent for him not to receive *Saerrath* (free wages) from any one but a king, but he is not entitled to refuse the free wages of his king. Every man in the *Tuath* is bound to receive wages of a *Rig Tuatha*."

All Ceiles, whether free or base, had certain definite rights in the territory, and had the right to have a habitation and the usufruct of the land. The free *Ceiles* paid *Bes Tigi*, or house tribute, the base *Ceiles*, *Biatid*. If a *Flath* exacted more *Biatid*, &c., than he was legally entitled to, he was bound to recompense his *Ceile* by additional wages. The *Saer Ceile* formed the body-guard of the chief. The *Daer Ceile* sometimes received benefices of land. In a lower position in the social scale were the *Bothacks* or cotters, the *Leu Cluthes* or house servants, and the *Fueders* or strangers, outdoor labourers; the latter were *Saer Fueder*, free labourers, and *Daer Fueder* or base, servile labourers. The *Daer Fueders* became tenants from year to year, but if they served for three generations they acquired rights to the possession of land. The *Flath* could have *Bothacks* or *Fueders* of any class on his land. The *Ceiles* alone had political rights, that is, a definite position in the tribe or *Tuath*. The *Bo Aire*, if wealthy, became a *Flath*. It is obvious that the main distinction lay between the "lineage," the members of the family, and strangers who had either been captured in battle, been purchased as slaves in England, or come amongst the sept in search of fortune. The *Ceiles* appear to have been part of the "lineage," and as such entitled to greater privileges than captives, slaves or aliens. This view is borne out by one of the most important ancient Irish documents, the *Crith Gablach;* it is in the form of question and answer; it relates to the classes of society, and their privileges among the ancient Irish. It commences,—

"What is Crith Gablach ?—Answer : The thing which the man of a tribe accumulates for his benefit in the territory till he is admitted to the rank of the legitimate possessors of the territory ; or other increase by which distinction is given to the grades of the people."

There is here an evident distinction between the "man of the tribe"—the lineage, and strangers. It appears that he should prove his worthiness by increasing the wealth of the tribe, and was then placed by the tanist among "the legitimate possessors of the territory," or receive other distinction. The grades of the people were "a Fer-Midbe, a Bo-Aire, an Aire Dessa, an Aire Tuise, an Aire Forgaill, and a Ri. They were ennobled by the possession of *Deis*-land, which was in the award of the tanist, and they ranked in the tribe and out of it, according to the rank which they won. The *Tanose Righ* (tanest of a king) was so called because he was elected by the whole territory. The seven lawful occupations of a King were—Sunday, ale-drinking, for he is not a lawful Flath who does not distribute ale every Sunday. Monday, at legislative government of the tribe ; Tuesday, at chess ; Wednesday, seeing greyhounds coursing ; Thursday, the pleasures of love ; Friday, at horse-racing ; Saturday, at judgment.

The *Flath* could either work his land with *Fueders*, or let it to *Ceiles*, but as his own holding terminated with his life, the lettings were usually of short duration. Any buildings became the property of the *Flath* at a valuation, but if evicted before the expiration of the term, the occupier was entitled to his buildings, and if evicted without cause he was entitled to his rent as well as his house. Tillage land, let for the purpose of growing a manured crop, reverted to the owner at the end of the term ; if no term was specified the hirer of the land was entitled to its possession, until he had exhausted the manure. With reference to the quantity of land attached to a dwelling-house he says (p. xxxix.)

" The Norse *Bo'l* and *By* appear to be synonymous ; at least there is no doubt that *By* originally was a mansion or principal farmhouse, including, of course, sufficient land to keep a family in independence. In Ireland this appears to have been the quantity of land sufficient to graze twenty-one cows or three cumals, the legal qualification of a *Bo Aire* of the lowest class, that is, of a free man having political rights, and in addition a certain quantity of forest, and sufficient meadow land to provide winter fodder. The following curious Irish entry in the Book of Armagh appears to represent such a typical homestead :—" Cummen and Brethan purchased Ochter-u-Achid with its appurtenances, both wood and plain and meadow, together with its habitation and its garden."

The annals of the Four Masters, a work of some authority, informs us that gold was smelted in Ireland and made into cups, brooches, &c., as early as 354 B.C., that cloths were dyed. Each rank was known by the number of colours in their garments, kings wearing six colours, while the peasantry were obliged to wear a dress of one colour. Rings and chains were worn by the kings and chieftains.

The Irish *Seisreach* was the extent of land which occupied one plough, and represented the ploughland or carracute of

England, and the Saxon "hide of land." According to a curious poem attributed to the antediluvian Fuitan, but which belongs in substance, though not in language, to about the sixth or seventh century, has been published by Professor O'Curry in his tract on the battle of Moylena, there were in Ireland 184 *Trincha Céds*; 5,520 *Baile Bialachs*; 22,080 *Caethranchadhs* or quarters; and 66,240 *Siesreacks*, or ploughlands, which would be equal to 132,480 *Ballybors*, or habitations of freeholders, or 7,948,800 Irish acres, the remainder, 5,000,000 acres, being bog or mountain. At present there are 325 Baronies, and 62,205 townlands, the average acreage of the latter being 324·6 acres.

I have already referred to the assemblage of the legislators by Ollamb Fodhla, and to the collection of the laws made by him; they are called the *Psalter of Tara*. Irish records also refer to the *Psalter of Cashel*. The annals of the Four Masters inform us that A.D. 266 Cormac collected the laws and formed them into a book known as the *Psalter of Teamhair*. It contained a survey of the land of Ireland, and articles relating to Irish laws, genealogy, history, topography, &c., and at a late period, at the suggestion of St. Patrick, the laws were again collected, and the *Seanchus and Feanchus*, (*i.e.*, history and law), now called *Senchus Mor*, or Cain Phadrig (Patrick's law) was compiled. It was esteemed of such authority that no individual Brehon dared to abrogate it. This collection of laws, though more recent than the others I have named, possesses great antiquity, and was compiled before either the Justinian or the Theodosian codes.

The work of the several assemblies appears to have been one of compilation or collection, rather than of legislation, and in this there is a close resemblance to the theocracy of the Israelites, who received a heaven-given law with strict injunctions to observe its dictates, but neither judges, priests, nor kings were authorized to alter its conditions. There was no such thing as a re-form Bill; the *form* of its enactments, its requirements, and its penalties were prescribed, and there was therefore no need of re-forming them. Legislation in Ireland appears to have been tribal, and to have rested upon patriarchal institutions; the system would be properly described by the words "customary law." The collection or codification which took place tended to secure uniformity over the whole country, but the highest officer, the *Rig Tuatha*, or king, was neither endowed with the right of legislation nor the power to enforce the laws. These privileges appertained to the sept or tribe which acted through its elected officers, the chieftain and tanist. The laws were expounded and explained by the Brehons, who appear to have possessed functions similar to those of the courts of equity, in applying to a new class of incidents the principles of existing legislation.

Much jealousy existed as to the ownership of these ancient psalters. They were preserved with the most watchful care, and classed among the choicest treasures.* The more recent

* AN ANCIENT PSALTER.—Fac-similes of Irish national MSS. are at present being selected and edited by Mr. Gilbert, of the Public Record Office of Ireland. The first part of the collection, which will be one of profound interest to Irish scholars, is nearly completed. We learn from a report just issued, that among the documents, fac-similes of which have been prepared, is a Latin psalter styled "Cathach," or the "Fighter." It is ascribed to the hand of St. Columba, who made Iona famous, and receives its name from the antique metal casket in which it is preserved. The legend is that, while sojourning with St. Finnen, in Ulster, he borrowed this psalter, and "copied it furtively in his church, with the aid of miraculous light, in the night-time." Finnen claimed the copy as his property, but Columba did not recognise his right, and King Diarmid was appealed to. His Majesty decided "that as to every cow belongs her calf, so to every book belongs its copy." Columba did not see the force of his analogical reasoning, and kept the treasure. The psalter was preserved as a sacred heirloom among his kindred the O'Donels, who ruled in the most western part of the north of Ireland, styled Tir Conaill, or the land of Conaill, from their progenitor of that name, and now known as Donegal. The present casket was made in the eleventh century by the direction of Cathbar O'Donell, head of the clan. It was long believed that if the Cathach was borne thrice before battle on the breast of a sinless cleric round the troops of the O'Donels, victory would be secured to them in a just cause. "To open the Cathach," says the report, "was thought unlawful, and would, it was thought, be followed by death and disasters among the O'Donels." It ultimately came into the possession of Daniel O'Donel, who raised a regiment in Ireland for James II,

of these law tracts is the Senchus Mor. Its text and a translation has been published by the commissioners appointed in 1852. It has formed the basis of Sir Henry Maine's justly celebrated "Essay on ancient institutions;" it is said to have been compiled by nine eminent men, a treble trinity, Kings, Brehons, and Prelates: King Laighaire, King Daire, King Core; Rossa, Duththack, Fergus; St. Benignus, St. Patrick, and St. Caernech. It is not my object to give you any description of this body of ancient Irish law, I only mean to deal with that portion relating to landholding. As I have already remarked, these law tracts do not either give or define the possession of land, nor do they allude to any rent except that which is called "food rent," to which I shall presently refer.

The transcripts were made by the late Dr. O'Donovan and the late Professor O'Curry, from law tracts in the Irish language in the libraries of Trinity College, Dublin, of the Royal Irish Academy, of the British Museum, and in the Bodleian Library at Oxford. The transcripts made by Dr. O'Donovan extend to nine volumes, comprising 2,491 pages, and the transcripts made by Professor O'Currey are contained in eight volumes, extending to 2,906 pages. They did not live to revise and complete their translations. The preliminary translation executed by Dr. O'Donovan is contained in twelve volumes, and the preliminary translation executed by Professor O'Curry in thirteen volumes.

They are now in course of publication under the title of the *Senchus Mor*, the great laws. Sir Henry Maine says of them,—

"The Senchus Mor, the great book of the ancient laws, was doubtless a most precious possession of the law school or family to

---

and afterwards became a brigadier in the French service. It remained on the Continent until 1802, when it was transferred to Sir Hugh O'Donel, of Newport, in the county of Mayo. In 1814 his widow began proceedings in Chancery against Ulster King of Arms, for having opened the Cathach without permission. The manuscript, it is said, now consists of fifty-eight leaves of vellum, many of which at the commencement are damaged.

which it belonged, and its owners have joined to it a preface in which a semi-divine authority is boldly claimed for it. Odhran, the charioteer of St. Patrick—so says the preface,—had been killed, and the question arose whether Nuada the slayer should die, or whether the saint was bound by his own principles to unconditional forgiveness. St. Patrick did not decide the point himself. The narrator, in true professional spirit, tells us that he set the precedent according to which a stranger from beyond the sea always selects a legal adviser. He chose to go according to the judgment of the royal poet of the men of Erin, Duththach Mac na Lugair, and he 'blessed the mouth' of Duththach. A poem, doubtless of much antiquity and celebrity, is then put into the mouth of the arbitrator, and by the judgment in it Nuada is to die; but he ascends straight into heaven through the intercession of St. Patrick. Then King Laighaire said, ' It is necessary for you, O men of Erin, that every other law should be settled and arranged as well as this.' 'It is better to do so,' said Patrick. It was then Duththach was ordered *to exhibit all the judgments and all the poetry of Ireland, and every law which prevailed among the men of Erin.* . . . This is the Cain Patraic, and no human Brehon of the Gaidhil is able to abrogate anything found in the Senchus Mor."

The manuscript from which the "Senchus Mor" is translated and published contains the following touching note:—

"One thousand three hundred two-and-forty years from the birth of Christ till this night; and this is the second year since the coming of the plague into Ireland. I have written this in the twentieth year of my age. I am Hugh, son of Conor M'Egrim, and whoever reads it, let him offer a prayer of mercy for my soul. This is Christmas night. I place myself under the protection of the King of heaven and earth, beseeching Him that He will bring me and my friends safe through the plague. Hugh wrote this in his father's own book in the year of the great plague."

Another of the manuscripts containing Irish law tracts has the following entry:—

"This is the eve of the great festival of Mary, and it grieves me that Donough O'Brien is in danger of death from the son of the Earl of Ormond, and it is a wonder to me that Cuirbre is courting council from Connor. The Park is my residence. Magnus for Domhnall and himself travelling, Eiri A.D. 1567."

These laws treat of the mode of recovering debts, and give the law of distress at considerable length, but they do not recite the origin of the division of land among tribes, or the subdivision among the members of the sept. There was, as I have already stated, no such relation as landlord and tenant, and I am informed that there is not a word in the Irish language which can fairly be translated to mean the Saxon derivative, "*a holding*," or the Latin derivative, *tenure* or *tenement*. The absence of any such words in the language is an indication that the Irish institutions only recognised one estate in land; in this it was in harmony with the institutions of the more ancient systems. The creation of two estates, the ownership or *quasi*-ownership, and the estate of use, was the invention of the Romans, and was adopted by those countries whose systems were moulded upon the jurisprudence of Rome.

I do not find in the "Senchus Mor" distinct indications as to the mode of distributing chattels, yet I am disposed to adopt Sir John Davis's view, that they went in gavelkind; but it seems that some men had cattle without land, while others had land without cattle; or the expression may be qualified by saying that one man had land in excess of his stock, while another had stock in excess of his land. Hence arose a sort of partnership, and the Brehon code deals at length with the circumstances arising from one man using the stock of another. These laws appear under two distinct heads, *Cain Saerrath* and *Cain Aigillne:* the former, as I am informed, means honour or personal relations, and the latter, "tribute or fine," and "forfeit." I am assured that there is nothing in the Irish words to justify the translation which appears in the preface as well as in the margin, "Saer-stock *tenure*" and "Daer-stock *tenure.*" The addition of the word "tenure" conveys an incorrect idea, and the writers of the preface, as well as Sir Henry Maine, who has adopted their views, have applied the word "tenure" to the land and not to the stock. There was undoubtedly a "holding" of the cattle, as they were rented or hired, but there was no claim upon the land in consequence of these relations. The writers of the preface to vol. ii., p. 49, thus describe the law:—

"In 'Saer'-stock tenure the chief gave the stock without requiring any security from the tenant. He gave it in consideration of receiving an annual return for seven years of one-third of the value of the stock given. The chief might claim this return in the form of manual labour at the time of the erection of his ' dun ' fort, or of the reaping of his harvest ; or if the chief did not need manual labour, he might require the ' saer '-stock tenant to attend him in a military expedition, and to send a man to do homage to him at the payment of rent."

This passage would read quite as well if the word "tenure" in the first line and tenant near the end were omitted : they suggest ideas with regard to the land quite at variance with the Brehon code. The stockholder held the stock, he was tenant of the stock, and paid rent or tribute for the stock, but none of these capacities affected his ownership of his lands.

The preface to vol. ii. of the "Senchus Mor," p. l., adds,—

"The principal Irish tenure appears to have been ' daer '-stock tenure, into which the tenant entered by choice, and in which he was required to give security for the stock he used. From the optional nature of the tenure, the law respecting it was called ' Cain Aigillne,' that is, the ' Cain ' law of options in tenure. The securities given were called ' Giallna ' securities, to distinguish them from kinsmen's securities. . . . . The ' Cain Aigillne ' contains traces of very careful provisions for guarding against the arbitrary termination by either chief or tenant of ' daer '-stock tenure when once entered into."

The laws appear to be based upon the principle of making the stock-borrower pay the stock-lender double food-rent for the year if he returned the stock without the consent of the lender, inasmuch as he might not have grazing-ground for the stock so returned. If the stock-lender recalled his stock the borrower was entitled to one-third of it, and was exempted from payment of his honour price ; otherwise his land might lie idle.

These arrangements did not in any way affect that which we understand by the word "tenure," that is, a man's farm, but they related solely to cattle, which we consider a chattel. It has appeared necessary to devote some space to this subject, inasmuch as that usually acute writer Sir Henry Maine has accepted the word "tenure" in its modern interpretation, and has built up a theory under which the Irish chief "developed" into a feudal baron. I can find nothing in the Brehon laws to warrant this theory of social Darwinism, and believe further study will show that the *Cain Saerrath* and the *Cain Aigillne* relate solely to what we now call chattels, and did not in any way affect what we now call the freehold, the possession of the land.

There is nothing in the *Senchus Mor* at all contradictory of the statements made by Spenser and Sir John Davis, that the *tanistry* system gave every member of the sept or tribe the life ownership of a portion of its lands; that the official lands attached to the position of Chieftain and Tanist were not divisible, but partook of the nature of a benefice, they went whole and undivided to the successor to the office, and I can find nothing to warrant the conclusion arrived at by Sir Henry Maine, that the chieftain could give strangers the lands of the sept. *Fosterage* was a portion of the tanistry system, and those who were adopted by the sept shared in its responsibilities and enjoyed a portion of the lands. The chieftain and tanist each enjoyed his lands for his own life, and therefore they had no power of giving them away; they were tilled by the *Fueders* or *Bothacks*.

After the Norman invasion, and during the unsettled state of the country, the chieftains may have imitated the example of the Norman barons, and striven to make for themselves a title similar to that imported into Ireland by the strangers, but I doubt if anything of this kind existed while the Brehon code was in full force, before the invasion of the Danes and the Normans.

The early Norman and English settlers denounced the tanistry system as barbarous and uncivilized, and acted towards it in the same manner as the English of recent times have acted towards the Hindoo and New Zealand land systems; in the former they have looked upon the Zemindar, and in the latter the chieftain, as enjoying the same rights as the feudal baron. The English in both these countries have done the same injustice to the inferior owners which their forefathers did to the inferior members of the Irish sept or tribe. Mr. Thornton, a writer whose very able works deserve the serious consideration of our statesmen and legislators, has shown the manner in which the estate of the ryots was, by mistaken legislation, transferred to a class who were mere tax-gatherers; and thus in India as in Ireland the sympathies of the mass of the people was estranged from British rule, the people regarded the invaders as spoliators, who had not only assumed the government, but deprived them of their rights. As I shall have to speak hereafter of these changes I shall not dwell on them now; but before I close this portion of my subject would like to give you some idea of the state of Ireland when the unmixed tanistry system prevailed. It was refined and elevated by the introduction of Christianity, but was not broken in upon until the incursions of the Danes.

The earliest missionaries are not known. The Irish traced their Christianity through Irenæus to St. John, thus carrying back their faith to the Holy Land; the bull of Pope Clementine to Palladius, who visited Ireland before the landing of St. Patrick, authorizes him to visit "our brethren in Christ in Ireland," thus asserting the previous introduction of Christianity. But it must have been confined to special districts, for there appears to have been a wide field for the labours of St. Patrick. It has, however, been a puzzle to learned men to discover how so many of the rites of the Eastern or Greek Church were implanted or existed in Ireland for many centuries. It is said, "If St. Patrick was the real founder of Irish Christianity, and was connected with the Latin Church, how does it come to pass that the Irish Church corresponded in its formulæ with the Greek Church, and why did it teach its rites in Scotland, England, and France?" I cannot solve this difficulty, but it seems to imply a settled church with established formulæ before St. Patrick's visit, and it is quite clear he did not disturb these usages, and that they continued for centuries after his death.

It had been the custom to misrepresent this system of landholding, and to describe it as barbarous and inequitable, but more recent inquirers, on the Continent as well as in England are beginning to take a different view, and to recognise the equity and humanity of the Brehon code. It may not be out of place to glance at the history of Ireland to ascertain what was the effect of the *tanistry* system, and of the laws regulating the possession of the soil. Land is a bond of union. Its produce satisfies man's physical wants. Its distribution is the basis of legislation. During the existence of tanistry, Ireland was the ark, in which the knowledge of the Western world rode secure amid the turmoil of the Gothic invasion. It was the school of learning for Western Europe. King Alfred was educated in Ireland, and it furnished the first masters to the Universities of Paris and Padua. The scholastic institutions of Bangor, in the county Down, and Lismore, in the county Waterford, educated thousands of pupils. Bangor alone is reported to have had five thousand students. The Irish missionaries visited and settled in the south of Scotland, the north of England, in France, and in Switzerland, where the memory of an Irish scholar is perpetuated in the name of St. Gall. Ireland gave bishops to Northumberland and to Germany, and she then received from Europe the title of "the Isle of Saints." One of her learned sons, Donatus, who succeeded Albinus as head of the college at Padua in the ninth century, left a Latin description of Ireland at that time:—

> "Far westward lies an isle of ancient fame,
> By nature blessed, and Scotia is her name,
> Enrolled in books; exhaustless is her store
> Of veiny silver and of golden ore;
> Her fruitful soil for ever teems with wealth,
> With gems her waters, and her air with health;
> Her verdant fields with milk and honey flow,
> Her woolly fleeces vie with virgin snow;

> Her waving furrows float with bearded corn,
> And arms and arts her envied sons adorn.
> No savage bear with lawless fury roves,
> No rav'ning lion through her sacred groves,
> No poison there infests, no scaly snake
> Creeps through the grass, nor frogs annoy the lake;
> An island worthy of its pious race,
> In war triumphant, and unmatched in peace."

The venerable Bede, in his history, tells of the munificence and liberality of the Irish. He says,—

"These visitors were most willingly received by the Scots [thus he terms the Irish], who maintained them at their own charge, supplied them with books, and became their teachers without fee or reward."

This passage of Bede should never be quoted without a recollection of the comment presented by Lord Lyttleton, who styles it "a most honourable testimony, not only to the learning, but likewise to the hospitality and bounty of the Irish nation."

John Sulgen, son of Sulgen who was Bishop of St. David's in the year 1070, thus describes the condition of Ireland, and their bounty towards strangers. He thus wrote in the life of his father:—

> "With ardent love for learning Sulgen sought
> The school in which his fathers had been taught;
> To Ireland's sacred isle he bent his way,
> Where science beamed with bright and glorious ray.
> But lo! an unforeseen impediment
> His journey interrupted as he went;
> For sailing toward the country where abode
> The people famous in the "word of God,"
> His bark, by adverse winds and tempests tossed,
> Was forced to enter on another coast;
> And thus the Albanian [Scotch] coast the traveller gained,
> And there for five successive years remained.
>   *   *   *   *   *   *
> At length arriving on the Scottish [Irish] soil,
> He soon applies himself to studious toil.
> The Holy Scriptures now his thoughts engage,
> And much he ponders o'er the oft-read page,
> Exploring carefully the secret mine
> Of precious treasure in the law divine;

> Till thirteen years of diligence and pains
> Had made him affluent in heavenly gains,
> And stored his ample mind with rich supplies
> Of costly goods and sacred merchandise;
> Then, having gained a literary name,
> In high respect for learning, home he came,
> His gathered store and golden gains to share
> Among admiring friends and followers there."

The late Rev. Arthur West Haddon, in an article upon the Scots (Irish) on the Continent, which will well repay perusal, speaks of the race of scholars, "who from the sixth to the tenth century went forth from Bangor and Lindisfarne upholding Greek learning and philosophic speculation, asserting the freedom of the will, believing in the existence of the Antipodes, by far the best astronomers of their time, who well nigh anticipated the theory of Copernicus. This remarkable and interesting school followed in the wake of St. Columbanus forming into famous societies at Luxeuil, St. Gall, and Bobbio, and branching off into minor foundations at Reichenau, Disentis, Remiremont, Lure, Jouarre, Faremoutier, Lagny, Hautvillers, Moutier-en-Der, Fontenelle, and Jumieges."

Mr. Haddon says of Ireland:

"In the gradual development of the Papal power she remained in her isolation a standing proof of the novelty of theories unknown to the Church in earlier times, a living instance of what had formerly been held for truth, an island not absorbed by the rising waters of the Papacy, until, indeed, the twelfth century."

A curious though well-authenticated discussion as to the position of the Irish nation occurred at the Council of Constance, A.D. 1414:—

"There was an ancient custom in those councils of voting by 'Nations,' as it was called. Four 'nations' were acknowledged—viz., France, Spain, Germany, and Italy. These 'nations' were not 'kingdoms.' Each was a collection of several independent kingdoms. They had the lists; and they found that each 'nation' comprised six or eight kingdoms, whose governments were independent of each other. At the Council of Constance, which was held A.D. 1414, the King of England claimed that the English should be acknowledged as a separate 'nation,' having a vote of their own in the council. The King of France was very jealous at this, and ordered his ambassadors to protest against it in the council; their

protest is given in the appendix of the council to which he had referred. The ambassadors insisted that England had always been reckoned part of the German 'nation' in all general councils; and they maintained that it ought to be so still, for, as England had only twenty-five bishops, it was absurd that so few should have a separate vote in the council. The ambassadors of the English king were heard in reply, and they did not deny either of the above statements; but they said, in answer to the fewness of their bishops, that the Irish, who had sixty dioceses, were united with them in the 'Anglican nation,' and taking in the Welsh, and some Scotch bishops who joined with them, there were 110 bishops altogether. And in answer to the statement that England had always been counted part of the German nation, and not a nation in itself, they did not deny it; on the contrary, they seemed to admit that this was true; but then they quoted St. Albert the Great and Bartholomæus as follows:—
'That the whole world being divided into three parts, viz., Asia, Africa, and Europe; Europe is divided into four kingdoms—first, the Roman; secondly, the Constantinopolitan; third, the kingdom of Ireland, which is now translated to the English; and the fourth, the kingdom of Spain. From which it appears that the King of England and his kingdom are of the most eminent and the most ancient kings and kingdoms of all Europe, which prerogative the kingdom of France cannot obtain.' Such was the defence of the ambassadors of England. They did not rest their claim upon the rights of England itself, but on her possessing the ancient rights of Ireland; and thus England obtained dignity in Europe and influence in Christendom by her union with Ireland. For this defence having been heard by the Council of Constance, they decided that England and Ireland united should vote and rank as a separate nation, thus giving them an influence in the council which the King of France sought to prevent, and which would have been wholly lost if England had stood alone. As an appropriate acknowledgment of England's obligation to Ireland, the 'Anglican nation' was represented in that council by 'Patrick, Bishop of Cork.'"

I have endeavoured as briefly as possible to convey a correct idea of the land system of this period, which comprised nearly eighteen centuries, and during the latter portion Ireland was renowned for its learning and civilization. The Irish people naturally revert to this portion of their history with pride and satisfaction, and later writers, both English and foreign, are disposed to do justice to the humanity and excellence of the Brehon code of laws and the *tanistry* system of landholding.

Part II.—The Scandinavian or Mixed Period.

The comparatively peaceful and prosperous state of Ireland which existed under the Tanistry system of landholding, the Brehon social code, and the sway of Christianity, was broken in upon by the incursions of the Scandinavian sea robbers. They were called Easterlings or Ostmen, and also Galls, or foreigners. Their piratical expeditions commenced about the end of the eighth century, and whilst they infested England and France, Ireland did not escape. Their first invasions were made in small parties, for the sake of plunder, and they were frequently repulsed. By degrees the invaders, either by force or treaty, obtained some small settlements. The Irish, though too prone to predatory attacks, had no national armament, no united force to meet the disciplined hosts thrown upon their shores. Ireland had enjoyed such a state of peace, that there were no fortified places, no baronial residences; and hence it was easily overrun and ravaged. But the people rallied, and waged a not unequal war with the invaders, who failed to establish a dynasty in Ireland, though they did so in Normandy and England. The aboriginal English succumbed to the Anglo-Saxon, but the Irish resisted and defeated the Danes.

The first shocks of their invasion fell with great severity upon a people without central government, as none of the chieftains could bring into the field a force numerically equal to that of the invaders, they were defeated in detail. The Irish chieftain and the Tanist were both elected by the sept which spontaneously upheld their authority; therefore there was no need of the feudal castle with its band of armed men. The services of the tribes were not compulsory. The Anglo-Saxon thanes, or earls, surrounded their dwellings with a moat or ditch, they were approached by a drawbridge, they were protected with a portcullis and gates, they were furnished with armed men, and from the lofty keep the watchman gazed with unwearied eye over the country in order to detect the approach of a foe and give timely warning of danger.

The Celtic chieftain needed none of these safeguards. The clans might have wars with neighbouring or other clans, and might engage in warlike expeditions, but the rights of individuals became so merged in the general interests of the clan as not to produce the evils which arose from the arbitrary rule of petty chiefs. This comparative confidence had its own peculiar evil; the country was unprotected, and when invaded, either by the Danes or the Normans, there were few fortified places to retard their march.

The rapidity with which these invaders overspread the nation is attributed by Sir John Davis to the absence of castles and fortified places. He wrote,—

"Though the Irishry be a nation of great antiquity, and wanted neither wit nor valour, and though they have received the Christian faith above 1,200 years since, and were lovers of poetry, music, and all kinds of learning, and were possessed of a land in all things necessary for the civil life of man, yet, strange to be related, they did never build any houses of brick or stone, some few poor religious houses excepted, before the reign of King Henry II., though they were lords of the Irish many hundred years before and since the conquest attempted by the English. Albeit when they saw us build castles upon their borders, they erected some few piles for the captains of the country, yet I dare boldly say that never any particular person, either before or since, did build any brick or stone houses for his private habitation, but such as have lately obtained estates according to the course of the law of England. Neither did any of them in all time plant any garden or orchard, settle villages or towns, or make any provision for posterity."

We have here the picture of a nation enjoying all that contributes either to the wants or luxuries of life, and yet in the enjoyment of laws which promoted such comparative justice that at a period when nearly the whole of Northern Europe was studded with fortified castles, the residences of spoilers and oppressors, the Irish people enjoyed their "poetry, music, and all kinds of learning;" they "possessed all things necessary for the civil life of man," and yet were free from the continued apprehension that some neighbouring lord would swoop from his eyrie, and seizing their lamb in his powerful talons, bear it to his hold. The debauch and riot which disgraced the baronial hall, and debased alike the knight and the man-at-arms, were unknown amid the purer life of the Celts, who, actuated by nobler purposes, cultivated their own minds and then became missionaries, carrying to the outer world the sublime truths of Christianity and philosophy.

In the year A.D. 795 the first attack of the Danes upon the coast of Ireland was made. They laid waste the island of Rathlin, off the coast of Antrim. In 798 they attacked the coast of Ulster, and in 802 set fire to the monastery of Iona, and destroyed many of the monks. In 807 they effected a landing in Ireland, and penetrated as far as Roscommon, which they then destroyed, laying waste the surrounding country. The French annals inform us that in A.D. 812:—

"The fleet of the Normans having attacked Ireland (the island of the Scots), after a battle had been fought with the Scots, and no small part of the Normans killed, returned home in disgraceful flight."

Father Walsh thus expresses his sorrow at the devastation of the Danes:—

"There was no monarch in Ireland now (the ninth century) but the saddest interregnum ever any Christian people had or heathen enemies could wish. No more king over the people but that barbarous heathen Turgesius. No more now the island of saints, nor mart of literature. No more Beauchun (Bangor) to be seen, but in ashes now a second time, all the holy monks thereof murdered by the cruel Danes, and buried under its rubbish. No more the monastery of Fionbaur, at Cork, at which 700 conventual monks, and together with them seventeen bishops, at one time wholly devoted themselves to a contemplative life. No more that wonderful cloister of all for angelical visions and communications under St. Mochada, at Ruthin first, and then at Lismore, containing no fewer than 100 of the most remarkable monks for sanctity that have ever been of any age or nation. No more the celebrated cells of Maghbile, or any at all of so many holy places echoing forth continually the praises of God. No more the renowned schools of Dundaleagthghlus, Armagh, Lismore, or Cashel. No more a university, or academy, or college of learning in all the land, nor foreigners coming to admire or study in them."

These cruelties of Turgesius were avenged by Olchoban Mac Knee, who was at first Abbot and Bishop of Emly, but was afterwards raised to the throne of Cashel or Munster. In 846 Emly was invaded, and the residence of the bishop attacked. This roused the spirit of the warlike bishop, who attacked and defeated Turgesius. The cruel chieftain gathered his adherents and again attacked and expelled the Primate, Foraina, and his clergy, and burned the place. He was attacked by Melsiachlin, King of Ireland, and defeated and killed. Colgan says that during the several invasions of the Danes, Armagh was six times plundered, twice laid waste, and thirteen times burned. Kells was five times ravaged and thirteen times burned. Kildare was ravaged fourteen times and burned ten times; Clomacnoise was burned eleven times and plundered twenty-three times; and Cork was ravaged five times and set fire to seven times.

In 853 the Norwegian Prince Amlave (whose name is also written Olaff or Auliffe) came to Ireland, accompanied by his brothers Sitiu and Ivar. One of them built Dublin, another Limerick, and the third Waterford. They became converts to Christianity, and Olaff, or Saint Olaff, gives his name to one of the parishes and a church in the city of Waterford.

In the beginning of the tenth century the power of the Danes received a check. Flan Sivima was then King of Ireland; he repeatedly defeated the Danes. The uncultivated lands began to be tilled again, and Christianity dared to show its face once more, and the seminaries of learning began to flourish with new vigour. Cormac, King of Munster, collected and compiled the Irish historical records, which are known as the *Psalter of Cashel;* and built the beautiful small church on the Rock of Cashel called Cormac's Chapel. In his reign the Northmen or Danes returned, and after his death they attacked Ireland with fresh vigour. Waterford, Cork, Lismore, and Agaboe first felt their fury. They again spread misery and desolation through various parts of the isle. During this century the war between the Irish and the Danes was waged with varying success, until at length they were defeated by Brian Boroimhe at the battle of Clontarf in 1014, at which he and his son Morogh, and his grandson Turlogh, were slain. Churches, schools, and other religious establishments were erected and rebuilt, roads and bridges were constructed through the country, and the public highways put into repair. The lands, too, which had been usurped by the Danes were restored to their original proprietors, the pagan foreigners being expelled from them.

The necessity of defending themselves from foreign invasion led to changes in the social system of the Irish, and to the disturbance of that order which prevailed for centuries. Force was required to repel force; hence organisms arose quite foreign to its ancient institutions. The existence of armed disciplined bodies which sprung from invasion fostered ambition that led to schemes of conquest and disorder. Those who had taken up arms to defend their rights became themselves aggressors. There was no sufficiently strong central authority to repress violence; hence disorder and confusion prevailed to a greater extent than formerly.

The presence of the foreign element acted like a cancer in the system, and led to the further interference of strangers, and unhappily the religious element played an important part in these transactions and aggravated the evil. The Irish Church maintained a semi-independent existence, and enjoyed until the twelfth century a ritual almost identical with the Eastern or Greek Church. The invaders, however, having an affinity to the Normans, placed themselves under the banner of the Latin Church. When William of Normandy secured the English throne he thrust aside the Saxon prelates, and placed Lanfranc, an Italian, in the see of Canterbury. The Danish settlers in Ireland, being of the same race as the Normans, seized upon the opportunity of winning foreign aid for themselves. The cities of Dublin, Limerick, and Waterford almost simultaneously elected bishops, but, instead of having them consecrated in Ireland or in connection with the Irish Church, they sent them to England, and thus established an Episcopacy in Ireland, not in connection with the Irish Church, and gave the see of Canterbury a pre-eminence over Armagh. Patrick, who was chosen Bishop of Dublin in 1074, went to England to be consecrated by Lanfranc, Archbishop of Canterbury, and made the following profession of obedience:—

"Whoever presides over others ought not to scorn to be subject to others, but rather make it his study humbly to render in God's name to his superiors the obedience which he expects from those placed under him; on this account I, Patrick, elected prelate to govern Dublin, the metropolis of Ireland, do offer thee, reverend father Lanfranc, Primate of Britain and Archbishop of the Holy Church of Canterbury, this charter of my profession; and I promise to obey thee and thy successors in all things appertaining to the Christian religion."

The submission of even a portion of the people in Ireland to the rule of the Norman, tempted William I. to invade Ireland, but death prevented the fulfilment of his intentions and delayed that event.

The period of Danish irruptions was, however, like the seedtime, in which, amid apparent defeat, the ploughshare and the harrow tore the social system asunder and sowed seeds destined to affect the entire future. Nor were other influences wanting. The Irish Church held, on various points, dogmas more in accordance with the Greek than the Latin Church, and some historians assert that the authority of the Roman Pontiff was not as implicitly acknowledged as in other parts of Western Europe. In Northumberland and in France the Irish missionaries were denounced for holding views different from those of the Latin Church. The Irish archbishops did not go to Rome for the pallia. Indeed, Cardinal Barnabo goes so far as to declare that the Irish, at this period, were schismatics. Some of the Irish ecclesiastics, who derived their orders from Canterbury, were desirous of securing greater apparent uniformity; and one eminent prelate died in Switzerland on his second visit to Rome to promote this object. These negotiations led to the visit of Cardinal Papire, or Papeson, who came to Ireland as Legate in 1148, and in 1151 summoned a council of 3,000 ecclesiastics, and four palls were solemnly received from the Pope by the Archbishops of Armagh, Dublin, Cashel, and Tuam. At the same time the celebration of Easter was adjusted according to the usage of the Latin Church. This was the natural outcome of the election of bishops by the Danes and their consecration by the Archbishop of Canterbury. Unfortunately, at this juncture, the pontifical tiara graced the brows of the only Englishman (Nicholas Brakespeare) who ever filled the highest office in that Church, and some historians assert that he went so far as to confer the sovereignty of Ireland upon the English monarch. I have seen what purports to be the Bull of Pope Adrian IV., in which he claims that all the islands upon which "Christ, the Sun of Righteousness, hath shone, belong, of right, to the see of St. Peter's," and proceeds to give Ireland to Henry II., on condition that he would "establish the rights of the Holy Roman Church and pay Peter's pence." Adrian IV. was elected Pope in the same year (1154) that Henry II. succeeded to the kingdom; the Papal Bull is dated 1155. Its authenticity is denied by some later Catholic writers, who say, even if it was issued, it became inoperative, according to canon law, as it was not acted upon within a year; but older authorities admit its authenticity and validity. Matthew of Westminster, an ancient writer, says :—

"About the same time, Henry, King of England, sending solemn ambassadors to Rome, requested Adrian (who had recently been made Pope, and whose favour he confidently hoped to obtain as being an Englishman) that he would license his entering Ireland in a hostile manner, and allow him to subdue that country and bring back its beastly inhabitants to holding the faith of Christ in a more seeming manner, and induce them to become more dutiful children of the Church of Rome, exterminating the monsters of iniquity that were to be found in the country, which request the Pope graciously complied with, and sent the monarch the following letter, granting the sanction desired."

Then follows the letter.

Matthew of Westminster adds :—

"King Henry, therefore, towards Michaelmas (of the same year, 1155), held a Parliament in Winchester, in which he treated with his nobles concerning the conquest of Ireland; but because the thing was opposed to the wishes of his mother the Empress (Matilda), that expedition was put off to another time."

Cardinal Pole, in a speech to Parliament in the reign of Queen Mary, 1554, said :—

"That as Adrian was an Englishman, the tendency to add to the power and dominion of England made him willingly accede to the request made by Henry's ambassadors."

Henry was occupied with his continental dominions, and became embroiled in the feud with the Church which eventuated in the murder of St. Thomas-a-Becket (the Archbishop of Canterbury). These events delayed the projected invasion. The Irish kings and chiefs were aware of Henry's intentions, and this knowledge may have brought about the events which subsequently took place. No just pretence could be assigned for such an invasion as Henry contemplated. Ireland was entirely independent, and except upon religious grounds there was not a pretext for such an outrage upon her nationality, but events were hurrying forward which led to the ultimate subversion of her institutions and the destruction of her independence.

The Scandinavian invaders did not, as far as I can discover, make any alteration in the system of land-holding. They ravaged and destroyed, but did not attempt to build up, and, with the exception of some seaports and cities, they do not appear to have acquired permanent territorial rights. The Irish Septs, with their Chieftains and Tanists, continued to own the land, and the Brehon Code was the basis of their legal system.

PART III.—THE NORMAN OR FEUDAL PERIOD.

IT happens not infrequently in political affairs that events of an apparently secondary character tend to promote primary objects unattainable by direct means. The opposition of the queen mother, the Empress Matilda, the indifference of the English nobles, and the feud with the Church, seemed to have put an end to Henry's design to add Ireland to his other dominions; but an event in no way connected with the main object brought about that which had seemed improbable and remote. Dermod MacMorrough, King of Leinster, whose tyrannical, profligate, and inhuman disposition made him an object of terror and hatred to almost every one who knew him, had provoked the vengeance of Roderick O'Connor, King of Ireland, who expelled him from his dominions, A.D. 1167, in consequence of his violent abduction of the wife of Tiernan O'Ruarc. This Irish version of the Iliad, led Dermod, whose immediate dependants had deserted him in the hour of his distress, to seek the aid of Henry. That monarch was in France, and Dermod followed him, claiming his aid, and promising that if he would restore him to his kingdom he would become Henry's vassal. Dermod was not king of Ireland, he was one of the subordinate kings, and having been guilty of crime, was lawfully expelled from his dominions. If he became vassal to Henry, that monarch would —supposing he legally stepped into Dermod's position—have been subordinate to the King of Ireland. But Henry, however desirous of reaching the object of his ambition, was personally unable to accompany Dermod to Ireland. Wishing to avail himself of the opportunity of gaining a footing for the English in Ireland, he gave Dermod the following letter :—

"Henry, King of England, Duke of Normandy, Aquitane, Earl of Anjou, &c.

"*Unto all his subjects, English, Normans, Welsh, and Scots, and to all nations and people being his subjects, greeting,*

"Whereas Dermod, Prince of Leinster, most wrongfully (as he informeth) banished out of his own country craved our aid, therefore for so much as we have received him into our protection, grace, and favour, whosoever within our nation, subject unto our command, will aid and help him whom we have embraced as our trusty friend for the recovery of his lands, let him be assured of our favour and licence in that behalf."

This document proves that Dermod only claimed to be "*Prince* of Leinster," and the aid to be given him was "*for the recovery of his land.*" Notwithstanding Henry's letters of license, Dermod did not for several months succeed in obtaining succour. At length he prevailed on Richard, Earl of Pembroke, generally called Strongbow, to espouse his cause, by promising him his daughter Effa or Eva in marriage, and with her the inheritance of the princedom. This bait was swallowed by Pembroke. According to Irish law, the princedom was an elective office, which Dermod could not bestow. Strongbow secured the aid of Robert Fitzstephen and Maurice Fitzgerald, Hervey of Mountmorris, and Maurice de Prendergast, on condition of ceding to them the town of Wexford with a large adjacent territory as soon as by their assistance he could be reinstated in his rights. The invasion of Ireland was, therefore, the act of private adventurers; and as Dermod could not legally give them more than he possessed himself, the gifts were liable to all Dermod's obligations in relation to the lands. Fitzstephen and Fitzgerald landed in 1170 with 390 men. Strongbow with Raymond le Gross followed, and landed in Waterford 23rd August, 1170. Leinster was overrun, Dublin was captured, and Dermod was restored to his princedom, which he did not long enjoy, his death taking place in May, 1171. It does not appear that he ever performed the act of vassalage, or that Henry, as his superior, bestowed the order of investiture, which was part of the feudal system. Strongbow assumed the principality of Leinster as the dower of his wife; this, though consonant with English feudal law, was contrary to the Brehon Code, and, had right prevailed, Strongbow's claims, and those of his followers, were subject to the obligations of that code, as they represented Dermod.

Henry became jealous of the rising power of Earl Strongbow, and he addressed the following inhibition to the English in Ireland :—

"We, Henry, &c., &c., forbid and inhibit that from henceforth no ship from any place in our dominion shall traffic or pass into Ireland, and likewise charge that all our subjects upon their duty and allegiance which are there shall return from thence to England before Easter next following, upon pain of forfeiture of all their lands, and the person so disobeying to be banished from our land and exiled for ever."

Strongbow, who did not wish to lose his English possessions, or to exchange them for those he acquired in Ireland, sent the following reply by Sir Raymond le Gros to Henry.

"Most puissant Prince, my dread Sovereign, I came into this land with your Majesty's leave and favour (as far as I remember) to aid your servant Dermod MacMorrough; what I have won with the sword, what was given me, I give you; I am yours, life and living at your command."

This answer appeased Henry; the Earl remained at the head of the English and native forces. But Henry was not satisfied with this acknowledgment of his position. He called his vassals around him and fitted out an expedition; and in October, 1171, he landed at Waterford with 500 knights and 4,000 men-at-arms.

Roger of Hovenden, a contemporary historian, gives the following account of Henry's proceedings in Ireland :—

"On the next day after the coming of the King of England to Ireland, namely, on Monday, October the 18th, the festival of St. Luke the Evangelist, he and all his armies proceeded to Waterford, an Episcopal city. And there he found William Fitz-Adholm, his brother, and Robert Fitz-Reinard, and certain others of his own family, whom he sent on before him from England. And there he stayed fifteen days (until there had come to him the kings and nobles of the country). And there came to him, by his own order, the King of Cork and the King of Limerick and the King of Ossy and the

King of Meath, and Reginald of Waterford, and almost all the princes of Ireland except the King of Connaught, who said that he was of right the lord of all Ireland. The King of England, however, could not by any possibility attempt to crush him in war at that wintry season, in consequence of the flooded state of the country and the rugged mountains and desert wolds that lay between them. Moreover there came to the King of England in the place above mentioned all the archbishops, bishops, and abbots of all Ireland, and they received him for king and lord of Ireland, swearing fealty to him and his heirs, and the power of reigning over them for ever, and thereupon they gave him their papers [in the form of deeds with seals attached], and after the example set them by the clergy the aforesaid kings and princes of Ireland did in like manner receive Henry, King of England, for lord and king of Ireland, and became his men, and swore fealty to him and to his heirs against all men."

Henry left Waterford for Dublin on the 2nd November, 1171, and arrived in that city on the 11th November. He remained in Ireland until the 17th April, 1172. No battle was fought while he was in the country. He was received by the Irish princes more as a protector and patron than an enemy. Henry assumed the title of Lord of Ireland, and departed without striking one blow, or building one castle, or planting one garrison. Such was the conquest (?) of Ireland by Henry II., which was as unjustifiable as it was inefficient.

Sir John Davis, Attorney-General in the time of James I., thus describes the excursion of Henry II. into Ireland:—

" He departed out of Ireland without striking one blow, or building one castle, or planting one garrison among the Irish; neither left he behind him one true subject more than those he found there at his coming over, which were only the English adventurers spoken of before who had gained the port towns in Leinster and Munster, and possessed *some slopes of land* thereunto adjoining, partly by Strongbow's alliance with the Lord of Leinster and partly by plain invasion and conquest. The part of this island which was occupied by the adventurers, consisting of a small district round Dublin, and some ports along the south and east coasts, was taken under the direct dominion of the King of England, placed under the feudal law, and organized on the feudal system; the rest remained in the jurisdiction of the native chiefs and under the Brehon or Irish law."

Roderic O'Connor, King of Ireland, who had expelled Dermod for his conduct towards O'Ruarc, Prince of Breffrey, refused at first to acknowledge Henry's sovereignty, but in 1175, four years later, he entered into a treaty with Henry, which commences in the following manner:—

"This is the final treaty agreed to at Windsor on the octaves of St. Michael's Day, in the year of grace 1175, between our Lord Henry, son of the Empress Matilda, King of England, and Roderic, King of Connaught, through the agency of Catholicus, Archbishop of Tuam, and Cantordes, Abbot of St. Brendan, and Master Laurence, Chancellor of the King of Connaught.

"To wit, that the King of England grants to the aforesaid Roderic his liegeman, King of Connaught, so long as he faithfully serves him, that he shall be a king holding under him and ready to serve him as his own man, and that he is to retain possession of his present territories, as firmly and peaceably as he held them before that our lord the King of England came into Ireland, paying him tribute; and that he is to have under his superintendence and jurisdiction the whole of the remaining part of the land and its inhabitants, so as that they shall pay their tribute in full to the King of England through his hand; and that they shall still enjoy their own rights, and that the present holders shall continue to hold in peace, so long as they remain faithful to the King of England, and pay him faithfully and in full their tribute and other dues which they owe him through the hand of the King of Connaught, saving in all things the privilege and honour of our lord the King of England and his 'own' [*i.e.*, the rights, &c., of King Roderic]."

The tribute consisted of one hide for every tenth head of cattle killed in Ireland. The king reserved to himself Dublin and its appurtenances, all Meath and Leinster, besides Waterford and Dungarvan, which had been the territories of Dermod, King of Leinster.

Roderic was King of Ireland, and the treaty proves that Henry limited his claims to that part of the land of Ireland of which Dermod MacMorrough was prince, and even in that portion Henry did not acquire any rights not possessed by Dermod, and the inferior estates of the chiefs and members of the clans were not disturbed by the proffered vassalage. The tribute levied on the rest of Ireland was a sort of black mail to avert injury, but the fact that Henry never visited Connaught or acquired possession of the land was pleaded in an action in Galway, in the reign of Charles I., when the jury found that Henry had not acquired those lands.

Ireland was, according to the Multifinan MSS., divided as follows for fiscal purposes :—

Munster	70	cantreds,	2,100	town lands,	16,800	carracutes.
Leinster	31	„	930	„	7,400	„
Connaught	30	„	900	„	7,200	„
Ulster	35	„	1,050	„	8,400	„
Meath	18	„	540	„	4,320	„
Total	184		5,520	„	44,120	„

Each carracute was about 120 acres, and this would make the grazing land 5,254,400 acres; the area under tillage in 1875 was 5,332,813 acres; the number of cattle then was 1,656,000; in 1848 it was 1,435,291. The tribute paid by Roderic O'Connor would make the number of cattle in Connaught 270,000, in 1841 it was 298,877. One of the reasons which conduced to Henry's ready reception by the Irish princes was the hope that it would tend to secure better order and tranquillity in the realm. Radulphus de Diceto, Dean of London, who flourished under King John, A.D. 1197, says:—

"When the people of Ireland saw how wholly the mind of the King of England was set upon promoting and establishing peace, he being one that neither countenanced evil deeds by indulgent treatment, nor issued hasty sentence of death against any man summoned by his edict, they came to him suing for peace."

Jan., 1172, Henry convened the Council of Cashel, of which Giraldus Cambrensis observes :—

"While the island was therefore thus silent in the presence of the king, enjoying a tranquil calm, the monarch, wisely influenced by a strong desire to magnify the honour of God's church and the worship of Christ in those parts, summoned a council of the entire clergy of Ireland to meet at Cashel."

Amongst the enactments are those for the payment of tithes, the honouring of churches with due devotion, and constant attendance at them, labouring by every means to reduce the state of the Church to the model of the Church of England. Some time after this council, King Henry sent to Rome to Pope Alexander III. a copy of the decrees passed at it and a copy of the deeds of submission to himself, as king and lord of the newly-acquired island which he had received from the archbishops and bishops, and the pontiff "by his apostolic authority confirmed to him and to his heirs the kingdom of Ireland according to the form of the deeds of the archbishops and bishops of Ireland." Pope Alexander wrote three letters, all bearing date the 20th September, 1172, one addressed to the prelates of Ireland, another to Henry II., and another to the Irish nobles. The first is addressed to Christian, Bishop of Lismore, legate of the apostolic see, Galasius, Archbishop of Armagh, and the archbishops and bishops of Ireland. He tells them that he is thankful to God for granting to Henry such a noble victory and triumph, and urges them to be very zealous in supporting a monarch who was so "magnificent a personage and so truly devout a son of the Church," and that they should assist him to the best of their power in retaining possession of the country, and if any of the kings, princes, or other people of the country should attempt to act in opposition to the oath of fealty they had made to King Henry, they, the bishops of the Church, were first to admonish him concerning his offence, and then, if their admonition were unheeded, to visit him with the terrors of ecclesiastical censure. "Be sure," says he, "that you execute our commands with diligence and earnestness, that as the aforesaid king, like a good Catholic and truly Christian prince, is stated to have paid to us a pious and benign attention in restoring you, as well the tithes as the other ecclesiastical dues, so you likewise may yourselves maintain, and as far as in you lies, procure that others shall maintain whatever privileges appertain to the king's dignity." The letter to King Henry praises him for his efforts to extend the power of the Church; he asks the king "to preserve to us in the aforesaid land the rights of St. Peter; and, even if the said Church have no such jurisdiction there, that your Highness should assign and appoint it for her." In the third letter to the Irish princes, he tells them how happy he had been to learn that they had wisely submitted to such a potent and magnificent king as their sovereign lord; a circumstance that promised their country, as he tells them, much greater peace, tranquillity, and improvement, and he exhorts them to be good subjects of King Henry, and to observe carefully the fealty and allegiance which they had promised on their oath to that prince.

In 1177 Henry II., having obtained license from Pope Alexander III., appointed his son John, King of Ireland in the presence of the bishops and peers, and in 1186 Pope Urban sent over two legates into Ireland to crown John, the king's son, there.

The relative value of Ireland and England in the reign of King John may be judged by the fact that when that miserable king by an instrument or charter granted to Innocent III. and his successors the whole kingdom of England and the whole kingdom of Ireland, and took back an estate thereof by an instrument sealed with a seal of lead, he undertook to pay 700 marks a year for England and 300 marks a year for Ireland. Ireland was then in point of inhabited houses considered to be to England in the ratio of two to seven. Ireland at the present day is to England in point of income as one to fourteen, though the population is about in the ratio of one to four. The recently published State papers, 1171 to 1251, do not contain any grant of land in Ireland during the reign of Henry II. Many were made in the reign of King John. The first, dated July

16, 1199, was made to the Knights Templars. It was followed by two grants to Walter Cross, one of the two islands of Asmudesty and Clere, for which the King received forty marks and the service of one and a-half knight's fee, the second gave one knight's fee at Karventhi and Kalke, two knights' fees at Kildeyn in the cantred of Huhene, and of five burgages within the walls of Limerick. Sept. 6 of same year there is a grant to Hamon de Valoignes of the two cantreds of Hochenel in the land of Limerick to hold of the King by the service of ten knights, and the same date a grant to Thomas Fitzmaurice of five knights' fees in the fee of Eleuri and cantred of Fontunel, and of five knights' fees in the fee of Huamerith in Thomond, on the river Shannon, and a burgage near the bridge on the left within the walls of Limerick. The same date there is a grant to William de Naas, of the castle of Karaketel, with five knights' fees in the fee of Syachmedth and cantred of Huhene and also of a burgage within the walls of Limerick. The same date a grant to William de Burgh of Aspatria, of the rest of the cantred of Fontunel, remaining in the king's hands, by the service of three knights' fees. The same date of a grant to Lambekin Fitzwilliam of a fee of five knights in the cantred of Hueme, and a burgage within the walls of Limerick, and the same day a grant to Robert Seignel of one knight's fee Chonchuherdechan, in the fee of Huerthern, and a further grant of four burgages within the walls of Limerick.

Sept. 12, same year, there are grants to Elyas Fitz-Norman, of the vill or adlongport, on the river Sur. To Humphrey of Tekeull of Kilduna, with three circumjacent knights' fees and a burgage in Limerick.

Sept. 12. Grant to Milo de Brit of twelve carracutes of land at Long in the fee of Othohel and cantred of Huheme. Then follow at intervals grants to Gerald Fitzmaurice, Geoffrey Fitzrobert, John de Gray, Hugh Hose, William de Burgh, the Knights Hospitallers, Meyler Fitzhenry, to the Cistercian monks, to Thomas Abbot of Glendalough, to the abbey and monks of Blessed Mary, in Mayo, to

Geoffrey de Costentus, Geoffrey de Marisco, Richard de Felder, and many others. In most cases a fine was paid to the king as well as the knights' service. Thus I find, Jan. 12, 1200, William de Breonne gives the king 5,000 marks that he may have the honour of Limerick. The king retains in his demesne the city of Limerick, the gift of all bishoprics and abbeys and all royalties, the cantred of the Ostmen and the Holy Isle, and the tenements and service of William de Burgh, three cantreds in Cork to hold by the service of ten knights. To Philip de Prendergast of forty knights' fees, of which fifteen were between Cork and Insovenoch. To William Marshall, Earl of Pembroke, of his land in Leinster, to hold by service of 100 knights. To Murad O'Brien of cantred in Thomond, and to Richard de Burgh of all the land of Connaught which William his father held of the King.

One of the early English settlers affords an instance of the way in which they were disposed to act towards the occupiers. Henry de Londres was not only Archbishop of Dublin and Papal Legate, but he was also Justiciary, an office equivalent to that of Lord Lieutenant. After his instalment as archbishop (1212) he summoned all the tenants and farmers of the see to appear before him on a day appointed, and to bring with them such evidences and writings as they enjoyed their holdings by. The tenants, at the stated time, presented themselves, and showed their evidences to their landlord, "mistrusting nothing;" but before their faces, on a sudden, he cast them all into a fire secretly prepared. This fact amazed some that they became silent, and moved others to a strong choler and furious rage that they regarded neither place nor person, but broke into irreverent speeches: "Thou an archbishop! nay, thou art a *scorch-villain.*" Another drew his weapon, and said, "As good for me to kill as be killed, for when my evidences are burned and my living taken away from me I am killed." The archbishop, seeing this tumult and imminent danger, went out at a back door; his chaplains, registers, and summoners were well beaten, and some of them left for dead. They threatened to fire the house over the bishop's head; some means were taken to pacify their outrage, with fair promises that all hereafter should be to their own content: upon this they departed. *See Ware's "Annals of Ireland."*

King John, as well as his son, Henry III., attempted to introduce English laws into Ireland, but their policy was frustrated by the barons, who preferred leaving the native Irish to be governed by their own laws and customs, which, being framed for a peaceful, contented people, gave more power to the invaders to persecute and oppress them; for, as the King's courts were not open to the Irish, who continued to be governed by the Brehon Code, the Normans could, if the blood of a relative was shed, plead that he was only an Irishman, and thus be secured from human vengeance. The unfortunate inhabitants, perceiving the advantage to be derived from English laws, petitioned Edward I. to admit them to the protection of British law, and offered him a purse containing 8,000 marks as an acknowledgment in return for the desired benefit. Twice they urged the appeal, and twice the king received it into favourable consideration, but evil influences prevailed, and the heartless rulers of Ireland succeeded in defeating the good intentions of the King and the just claims of an oppressed people, and in 1315 "Donald O'Neyl, King of Ulster and rightful successor to the throne of all Ireland, and the princes and nobles of the said land, as well as the Irish people," addressed Pope John XXII. They say,—

"That Pope Adrian, an Englishman, at the false suggestion of Henry II. made over to him the dominion of our realm," they add, " we were despoiled of our royal honour without any offence of ours, and handed over to be lacerated by teeth more cruel than those of any wild beasts." " For since that time when the English, upon occasion of the grant aforesaid, under the mask of a kind of outward sanctity and religion, wickedly crossed the borders of our realm, they have endeavoured with all their might, and with every act of treachery they could employ, to exterminate and completely to eradicate our people from the country, and by means of low crafty scheming they

D

have so far prevailed against us, that expelling us violently, without regard to the authority of any superior, from our spacious habitations and patrimonial inheritance, they have forced us to repair, in the hopes of saving our lives, to mountainous, woody, swampy, and barren spots; and exerting themselves to the utmost of their power to drive us from them, and to seize upon every part of our native soil for themselves, contrary to all right ; falsely asserting, in the extreme frenzy which blinds them, that we have no right to any free dwelling-place in Ireland, but that the whole property of the said country belongs entirely of right to themselves."

The document goes on to expose the treatment which the Irish received, and begs the Pope to appoint Edward Bruce to be king over them, and prayed that, out of a regard to justice and public tranquillity, the Pope would "forbid the King of England and our adversaries to molest us for the future; or, at least, kindly vouchsafe to execute for us upon them the due requirements of justice." The Pope, on receiving this appeal, addressed a remonstrance to King Edward, in which he reminds him that God hears the groans of the oppressed, and urges the expediency and advantage which would arise to the king from his looking into the wrongs of the Irish and granting them redress, so as to cut off all occasion of just complaint.

The Irish princes and nobles also complained to Pope John XXII. of the exclusion of Irishmen from positions in the Church, and referred to the decree of the Council of Kilkenny, which totally excluded all Irishmen from ordination or admission into the religious bodies.

The inhabitants were classified by the Duke of York, in his despatches to Richard II., as follows :—

"1st. Liegemen, or good subjects. 2nd. Irish enemies who had never submitted to the government, and who were, indeed, in a state of almost constant warfare with it. 3rd. Rebels, who, from being subjects by birth and submission, had taken up arms against the State, or at least renounced English laws and institutions."

In the reign of Henry III. the rights of ladies with regard

to the succession to land became the subject of legislation, and an Act was passed (14 Henry III.) which says,—

"Henry, King of England and Lord of Ireland, &c., &c. Certain knights of Ireland have made application to the king respecting *the descent of land* to sisters in Ireland, whether the younger sisters should do homage to the elder sister or to the king. The reply was, that by the custom of England they held as co-partners, and each should do homage to the king; and it enacts that this custom shall be proclaimed throughout our dominion of Ireland, to be straitly kept."

The sovereign tried to check the lawlessness of the English settlers and the king's officers; but as their object was to obtain the lands of the Irish people, the statutes of the sovereign became a dead letter. The 17th Ed. II., A.D. 1323, enacts,—

"1. That the king's officers shall not purchase lands in Ireland without licence; and if any do the contrary, it shall forfeit to the king and his heirs.

"2. That they shall not by colour of their offices take victuals of any person against his will.

"3. That they shall not arrest ships or other goods of strangers or our own people, but that all merchants and others may carry their corn and other victuals and merchandises forth of our realm of Ireland into our realm of England, and unto our land of Wales, under penalty of double damages, and shall also be grievously punished by us."

Edward IV. sought to break down the existence of the clan or sept, which, as equitable owner of the land of the tribe, continued to maintain its existence, and a law was passed in the fifth year of his reign, which sought to abolish the clan names. It enacted,—

"That the Irish dwelling amongst the English in the counties of Dublin, Moth (Meath), Urul (Louth and Monaghan), and Kildare, should no longer be called by the name of their sept or nation, but each one should take upon himself a several surname, either of his trade or faculty, or of some quality of his body or mind, or of the place where he dwelt, so as every one to be distinguished from the other."

It is not my object to write a history of Ireland, or to give any account of the unhappy incidents which arose from the weakening of the ancient system of laws and the absence of a competent jurisdiction. Sir John Davis, whose leanings were towards the English, observes,—

"Though Henry II. had the title of sovereign and lord over the Irish, yet did he not put those things in execution which are the true marks of sovereignty. For to give laws unto a people; to institute magistrates and officers over them; to punish and pardon malefactors; to have sole authority of making war and peace, and the like, are true marks of sovereignty, which King Henry II. had not in the Irish countries; but the Irish lords did still retain all these prerogatives to themselves; for they governed their people by the Brehon law; they made their own magistrates and officers, they pardoned and punished all malefactors within their several countries; they made war and peace one with another without controlment, and this they did not only during the reign of Henry II., but afterwards in all times, even until the reign of Queen Elizabeth."

The only object of the English appears to have been to acquire territories for themselves, and few crossed to Ireland except rude and barbarous warriors. The English adventurers and the colonies planted, took land from the Irish, yet they, as well as the Irish, strove to be independent of the Crown, and rose frequently in rebellion. In this state of disturbance many of the Irish were anxious to obtain the protection of English laws. The Brehon Code did not impose capital punishment, and if an Englishman murdered one of the *mere Irish* he claimed to be tried by Brehon law; while, if an Irishman murdered an Englishman, it was avenged with the utmost rigour.

"As long as they (the Irish) were out of the protection of English law," says Sir John Davis, "so as every Englishman might oppress, spoil, and kill them without controlment, how was it possible they should be other than outlaws and enemies to the crown of England? If the king would not admit them to the condition of subjects, how could they learn to acknowledge and obey him as their sovereign? When they might not converse or commerce with any civil men, nor enter into any town or city without peril of their lives, whither should they fly but into woods and mountains, and there live in a wild and barbarous manner? For, in a word, the English would neither in peace govern them by law, nor in war *root them out by the sword;* must they not needs be pricks in their eyes and thorns in their sides till the world's end?"

Where such a writer as Sir John Davis speaks of "rooting out an entire people with the sword," we may easily fancy the feeling that actuated more ignorant and barbarous men. The object of the adventurers was to acquire the lands of the Irish; they were harassed and tormented. Maurice Fitzthomas, of Desmond, began that system of extorting coin and livery, called in the old statutes a *damnable custom*, the imposing and taking of which, was made high treason.

"Besides," says Davis, "the English colonies being dispersed in every province of this kingdom, were enforced to keep continual guards upon the borders and marshes round about them, which guards consisting of idle soldiers were likewise imposed as a continual burthen upon the poor English freeholder and tenants, the great English lords and captains had power to impose this charge when and where they pleased; many of the poor freeholders were glad to give unto these lords a great part of their lands to hold the rest free from that extortion; and many others, not being able to endure that intolerable oppression, did utterly quit their freeholds and returned to England. By these means the English colonies grew poor and weak, though the English lords grew rich and mighty; for they placed Irish tenants upon the lands relinquished by the English, upon them they levied all Irish exactions, with them they married and fostered, and made gossips; so as within one age the English, both lords and freeholders, became degenerate and more Irish in their language, in their apparel, in their arms and manner of fighting, and all other customs of life whatsoever."

This sad picture shows how a noble people, intelligent and highly cultivated, sunk under tyranny and oppression.

One of the Lord Deputies, in the reign of Henry VIII., gives the following picture of that portion in the possession of the English:—

"The Pale is overrun with thieves and robbers. The soldiers so beggarly that they could not live without oppressing the subjects. Leinster was harassed by the Tooles, Burns, &c., but especially the county of Kilkenny was almost desolate. Munster, by the dissensions between the Earls of Desmond and Ormond, was almost ruined. Connaught was almost wasted by the feuds between the Earl of Clanricarde and McWilliam Oughton, and Ulster was in open rebellion with Shan O'Neil."

One of the State Papers addressed to King Henry VIII. about the year 1515, thus describes the land of Ireland,—

"If the land of Ireland were put once in order, it would be none other than a very paradise, delicious, of all pleasaunce in respect and regard of any other land in this world. Inasmuch as there was never stranger or alien person, small or great, who would avoid therefrom by his will, notwithstanding the misorder, if he might have the means to dwell therein. How much more would be his desire to dwell therein if the land were once put in order."

The putting in order which appears to be contemplated was the handing over to the English settlers the land of the Irish owners. The history of landholding in Ireland is almost an unvarying tale of spoliation.

Absence from Ireland was sufficient to forfeit lands held in that country. The condition upon which these lands were held implied residence, for it was found necessary, in the reign of Henry VI.,* to pass an Act by which such lands would not be forfeited in cases in which the person was employed upon the king's business.

* The 25th Henry VI., cap. 2, and 25th Henry VI., cap. 9, runs thus, "Also it is ordained and agreed that if any of the King's liegemen or officers of his land of Ireland be out of said land of Ireland by the commandment of the King or his Heirs, Lieutenants, their Deputies, Justices, or the King's Council of Ireland, that their lands, Tenements, Rents, Benefices, or Offices, or other possessions whatsoever, by their said absence shall not be seized or taken into the King's hands or his heirs, nor their offices void; and if so fortune that any of the said officers be taken by pirates or any other ill-doers or enemies, that they, at their return may occupy their said offices, notwithstanding any grant or gift of the said offices made to any other person in their absence, and if any service or gift be made to the contrary, the same shall be void and holden for none."

The English settlers, the descendants of the Norman barons, became less and less civilized, and they were described in the language *Hibernis ipsis Hiberniores*, more Irish than the Irish themselves. Rapine, injustice, and spoliation were the rule of these lords; and suffering, misery, and destitution the lot of the Irish people, who were deprived of the privilege of the mild laws of the Brehon code, which were unable to control Norman violence, and who did not receive the compensating advantage of the English common law; and the difficulties of the Irish were aggravated by an enactment which made the head of the sept answerable for every one of the sept, and bound him to produce him when charged with treason, felony, or any other heinous crime; thus the innocent were made to suffer with the guilty, and the lands of the whole sept were liable to fine for the non-apprehension of one of the real or supposed members of the sept. They were punished without trial, judgment preceded inquiry, and innocence and guilt were confounded in indiscriminate retribution.

Henry VIII. altered the title borne by his predecessors, and by an Act passed in the thirty-third year of his reign, that monarch took "for himself, his heirs and successors, the style and title of King of Ireland." The Act provided that "the king shall enjoy that style and title and all other royal pre-eminences, prerogatives, and dignities, as are united and annexed to the imperial crown and realm of England." Yet the Irish asserted their rights to their land, for Spencer relates:—

"That the Irish have always preserved their own law, which is the Brehon law, and that at the Parliament held by Sir Anthony St. Leger, Lord Deputy in the reign of Henry VIII., the Irish lords in acknowledging Henry for their sovereign reserved unto themselves all their former titles, tenures, privileges, and seigniories invalidate, and that their ancestors had no estate in any lands, seigniories, or hereditaments longer than during their own lives, for all the Irish do hold their land by tanistry, which is no more but a personal estate for his life, that is tanist, by reason that he is admitted thereunto by the election of the country."

Henry VIII. appears to have grappled very resolutely with one of the evils of English rule—the non-residence of the nobles. This, though the subject of previous legislation, was not enforced with vigour, but an Act in relation thereto was passed in the twenty-eighth of his reign, which is so quaint in its language, and so descriptive of the state of Ireland, that I quote its preamble at length.

28th Henry VIII., c. 3.—Forasmuch as it is notorious and manifest that this the King's land of Ireland heretofore being inhabited, and in due obedience and subjection to the King's most noble progenitors, Kings of England, who in those days in right of the crown of England had great possessions, rents, and profits within the same land, hath principally grown into ruin, desolation, rebellion, and decay, by occasion that great dominions, lands, and possessions within the same land as well by the King's grants as by course of inheritance and otherwise descended to noblemen of the realm of England, and especially the lands and dominions of the earldoms in Ulster and Leinster, who having the same both they and their heirs by process of time dwelling within the said realm of England, and not providing for the good order and surety of the same their possessions there, in their absence and by their negligences suffered those of the wild Irishmen, being mortal and natural enemies to the Kings of England and English dominion, to enter and hold the same without resistance, the conquest and winning thereof in the beginning not only cost the king's said noble progenitors charges inestimable, but also those to whom the said lands were given, then and many years after abiding within said land nobly defended the same against all the King's said enemies, and also kept the same in such tranquillity and good order as the Kings of England had due subjection of the inhabitants there, the laws obeyed and of their revenues and regularities were duly answered, as in any other where within the realm of England, and after the gift or descent of the said lands, possessions, and dominions to the persons aforesaid, they and their heirs absented themselves out of the said land of Ireland dwelling within the realm of England, not pondering nor regarding the presentation thereof, the towns, castles, and garrisons appertaining unto them fell in ruin and decay, and the English inhabitants there, in default of defence and justice and by compulsion of those of Ireland were exiled, whereby the said king's progenitors lost as well their dominions and subjections there, as also their revenues and profits and their said enemies by re-adopting or attaining the said lands, dominions, and possessions were elevated into great dominion, power, strength, and puissance for the suppressing of the residue of the king's subjects of this land which they daily ever since have attempted, whereby they from time to time usurped and encroached upon the king's dominions, which hath been the principal cause of the miserable estate wherein it is at the present time, and those lands and dominions by negligence and in default of the very inheritors, after this manner lost may be good example to the King's majestie now being intending the reformation of this land, to foresee and prevent that the like shall not ensue hereafter. It enacts that the lands of Thomas Harvard, Duke of Norfolk, and Lord Berkely, his co-partner in Carlow, Old Ross, and other manors; those of George Talbot, Earl of Waterford and Salop in Wexford, and the heirs general of the Earl of Ormonde; the Abbot of Furness; the Abbot of St. Augustine's, Bristow; the Prior of Chad Church, Canterbury; the Prior of Lanthony; the Prior of Cartmel; the Abbot of Kentisham; the Abbot and Prior of Oswy; the Abbot and Prior of Bath, and the Master of St. Thomas Acres, should forfeit their lands to the king, saving the right of all such as dwell in the land except those named, and saving also the right of John Barnewall, Lord Trimleton, and Patrick Barnevale.

Mr. Smith, in his work on the Irish, alludes to the following curious circumstance. He says (p. 100),—

"In the reign of Queen Mary, when the septs of O'More and O'Connell were attainted, the septs pleaded that the chieftain could not by attainder forfeit the septs' lands, which he had never possessed. It would perhaps have been difficult at that time in the case of any of the great forfeitures to meet this plea. A feeling that the land was still theirs, and that they were unjustly kept out of their possessions, seems long to have survived these vast confiscations in the minds of the *native proprietors*."

This shows that the system of Tanistry was continued in Ireland, and that the obligation imposed upon the sept and Crown were quite different from those which existed between liegeman and lord under the feudal system. The latter was a mutual tie of dependence and support; while the chief of the sept was merely an elected officer, and did not possess the land of the clan.

A review of the four centuries that elapsed from the landing of the English to the accession of Queen Elizabeth leaves upon the mind the impression of evil unmitigated by a single tint of good. The landing of the English cannot be elevated into the ranks of conquest, inasmuch as it took place upon the

invitation of a wicked prince, to reinstate him in the
dominions from which he had been evicted for his crimes.
The English monarch accepted a subordinate position as an
Irish Prince or chieftain, and despoiled his own subjects.
The acquisition of part of Ireland added no lustre or strength
to the English Crown; on the contrary, like all great
crimes, it brought its own punishment, and was a source of
weakness. It opened a field for truculent English nobles,
who, uncurbed by the sovereign, waged petty wars with the
Irish for the purpose of despoiling them of their lands. The
Barons became rebels. The Irish became disorganised, the
clans were forced into a warlike position quite foreign to the
genius of the Brehon code, in defence of their possessions, and
the chiefs placed at the head of armed forces imitated the
evil example of the English barons, and tried to acquire the
hereditary right over the joint property of the sept. Two
systems of jurisprudence prevailed, yet neither had the full
support of the administrative power of the Crown. The
Irish were refused the advantages of education, and forbidden to minister in the Church. The object of the
governors was spoliation; the adventurers lusted for the possession of the lands of Ireland; and as there could be neither
rebellion nor forfeiture where there was neither authority nor
obligation, the Norman invaders resorted to brute force;
"*lauv lauder cnaughter*," "the strong hand uppermost,"
became the motto of one of the most influential of the
English families, and swayed the policy of all the others. To
this was superadded the bitterness of religious strife, the
aid of foreign power was evoked by the rebellious English
subjects of the Queen. The Desmonds, the Geraldines, and
the De Burghos rose against the Crown, and sought not only
the aid of the more powerful Irish chieftains, such as the
O'Neils, but also that of Spain. An army landed in the
south, and it required 20,000 English troops to subdue
Ireland. The Crown seized upon the lands of its own
subjects, and Elizabeth rewarded Sir Walter Raleigh,
Edmund Spencer, and others by the gift of forfeited lands.

But the Irish executive did not wish for order or peace, and one of Elizabeth's ministers is stated by Lascelles, in *Res gestæ Anglorum in Hibernia*, to have said,—

"Should we exert ourselves in reducing this country to English order and civility it must soon acquire power, wealth, and consequence. The inhabitants will thus be alienated from England; they will either cast themselves into the arms of some foreign power, or perhaps cast themselves into a separate and independent state. Let us rather connive at their disorders; for a weak and disordered people can never succeed in detaching themselves from the crown of England."

True policy would have suggested a different mode of proceeding. Elizabeth's favourite scheme was that of repeopling it by an English colony; she issued letters to every county in England, encouraging younger brothers to become undertakers in a plantation of Ireland. The forfeited lands of the Desmonds were 574,628 acres, of which 244,080 were granted to the undertakers, and the remainder were restored to such of the former possessors as had been pardoned; but leases were made to the native Irish tenantry, and thus those whom Elizabeth wished to settle in Ireland defeated her intention, and instead of resident proprietors they became absentee middlemen."

Four Acts, the 11th, 13th, 27th, and 28th of Elizabeth, were passed for the purpose of confiscating the lands of the O'Neil in Ulster, those of the Knight of the Valley in Munster, of the White Knight in Munster, and of Viscount Baltinglass and the Desmonds in Leinster.

Spenser, who lived for some years in Ireland, thus speaks of the country:—

"And sure it is yet a most beautiful and sweet country as any under heaven; being stored throughout with many goodly rivers, replenished with all sort of fish most abundantly; sprinkled with many very sweet islands and goodly lakes like little inland seas, that will carry even shippes upon their waters, adorned with goodly wood, even fit for building houses and shippes, so commodiously, as that if some princes in the world had them, they would soon hope to be lords of the sea and ere long of all the world; also full of good ports and havens, opening upon England, as inviting us to come unto them, to see what excellent commodities that country can afford; besides the soil itself most fertile, fit to yield all kind of fruit that shall be committed thereto, and lastly, the heavens most mild and temperate, though somewhat more moist in the parts towards the west."

Ireland was invaded by the English for the avowed purpose of improving the condition of the people of the country; it had been held for about four hundred years, and let us ask, what was its condition? what were the benefits it received? The principal witness I shall produce is an Englishman, the gentle author of the "Faerie Queene," who by the gift of Queen Elizabeth became an Irish settler, and resided for many years upon the borders of the counties of Cork and Waterford. He says:—

"Notwithstanding that the same was a most rich and plentiful country, yet they were brought to such wretchedness as that any stony heart would rise at the same. Out of every corner of the woods and glens they came creeping forth upon their hands, for their legs would not carry them; they looked like anatomies of death; they spake like ghosts crying out of their graves; they did eat the dead carrions, happy when they could find them, yea, and one another soon after, insomuch as the very carcases they spared not to scrape out of their graves; and if they found a plot of watercresses or shamrocks, there they flocked as to a feast for a time, yet not able to continue there withal, so that in short space there was none almost left, and a most populous and plentiful country suddenly left void of man or beast."

Nothing can be more sad than this picture of the state of Ireland. The same writer in 1596 added,—

"There have been divers good plots devised and wise counsels cast already, about the reformation of that realm of Ireland. But they say it is the fatal destiny of that land, that no purposes whatsoever which are meant for good will prosper or take good effect."

Spenser thus recommends husbandry:—

"Because by husbandry, which supplieth unto us all things necessary for food, whereby we cheerfully live, therefore it is to be first provided for. The first thing, therefore, we ought to draw these new tithing men to ought to be husbandry. First, because it is the most easy to be learned, needing only the labour of the body, next, because it is most natural; and lastly, because it is the enemy to war and most hateth unquietness; as the poet saith,—

* * * "Bella execrata colonis;"

for husbandry, being the nurse of thrift and the daughter of industries and labour, detesteth all that may work her scath, and destroy the travail of her hand, whose hope is all her lives, comfort unto the plough."

As to the increase of cattle in Ireland he says,—

"I would, therefore, wish that there were some ordinance made amongst them, that whosoever keepeth twenty kine should keep a plough going, for otherwise all men would fall to pasturage and none to husbandry, which is a great cause of the dearth now in England, and a cause of the usual stealths in Ireland. For look into all countries that live in such sort by keeping of cattle, and you shall find that they are both very barbarous and uncivil, and also greatly given to war. The Tartarians, the Muscovites, the Norwegians, the Goths, the Armenians, and many others do witness the same, and therefore, since now we purpose to draw the Irish from desire of war and tumult, to the love of peace and civility, it is expedient to abridge their great custom of herding, and to augment their trade of tillage and husbandry."

The State Papers describe the condition of Ireland in the following language (vol. ii., p. 14):—

"What common folk in all the world is so poor, so feeble, so evil beseen in town and field, so bestial, so greatly oppressed and trodden under foot, fares so evil with so great misery, and with so wretched life as the common folk of Ireland? What pity is here wherewith to report! there is no tongue that can tell, no person can write. It passeth far the orators and Muses all to show the violence of the nobles, and how cruel they entreat the poor common people. What danger it is to the king against God to suffer his land, whereof he bears the charge and the cure temporal, to be in the said misorder so long without remedy! It were more honour to surrender his claim thereto, and make no longer prosecution thereof, than to suffer his poor subjects always to be so oppressed, and all the nobles of the land to be at war within themselves, always shedding of Christian blood without remedy. The herd must account for his fold, and the king for his."

The effect of the injustice which had been perpetrated and heaped up with continuous and increasing violence upon the Irish people was most deplorable. The confiscation of their land embittered their minds, and drove them into hostility to government. The refusal to admit the Irish to holy orders deprived the Church of the power and influence which it might have used to repress injustice and to soften the lot of those who were exposed to it. The constantly recurring rebellions of the Anglo-Norman nobles, who threw off the power of the Crown and assumed the title and state of princes, the wars between the Desmonds, Geraldines, and Butlers, tended to create and aggravate the confusion. The consequence of ill treatment was the degradation of the native race, it became demoralized and degraded. I cannot do better to illustrate their position than quote the words of Edmund Burke, who wrote,—

"To render men patient under the deprivation of all the rights of human nature, everything which could give them a knowledge or feeling of those rights, was nationally forbidden. To render humanity fit to be insulted, it was fit that it should be degraded."

Elizabeth had a long and most severe struggle to establish her authority in Ireland, and at the end of a war of upwards of seven years' duration, in which as many as 20,000 English troops were engaged, a final capitulation was agreed upon, but she did not live to see it perfected; it was signed a few days after her death. The country, worn out with this long and tedious war, was at length prostrate at the foot of the sovereign. The Plantagenets left to a new dynasty the duty of reconstruction and restoration, and we shall see how that trust was fulfilled.

PART IV.—THE STUART OR CONFISCATION PERIOD.

AFTER the rebellion and assassination of Shane O'Neil, 1568, his estates and those of his adherents, being most of the seignories and counties of Ulster, were confiscated by the 11th Elizabeth, c. i., 1569, and vested in the Crown. The lands were given to English adventurers, but they found it impossible to hold their ground against the original inhabitants. In 1588 O'Neill, the Earl of Tyrone, and other lords of Ulster, entered into a combination to defend their lands and religion. This war lasted fifteen years, and terminated in 1603. No cruelties were spared by the Lord Deputy Mountjoy to put them down. He made incursions on all sides, spoiled the corn, burnt all the houses and villages, and the people were reduced to live like wild beasts. Ireland, which had a population of two millions, was reduced to one-half. "The multitude," says Sir John Davis, "being brayed as it were in a mortar with sword, famine, and pestilence together, submitted to the English Government." All commodities had risen in value: wheat had advanced from 36s. to 180s. per quarter; oatmeal, from 5s. to 22s. per barrel, and other things in proportion. The submission in 1603 led to the settlement of Ulster by James I.

In 1586 the large estates of the Earl of Desmond in the counties Cork, Limerick, Kerry, Waterford, Tipperary, and Dublin, comprising 524,628 acres (statute measure), were escheated, not for any overt act of treason, but on account of his quarrels with the Earl of Ormonde. These large possessions were a strong temptation to the Irish governors, but they found some difficulty in passing a bill of attainder. A claim was also set up by the Crown to the whole of Connaught and the county Clare, and an arrangement was made with the Lord Deputy, Sir John Perrott, that the lords and gentlemen of that district should surrender them to the Crown and receive back, Royal Letters Patent. The surrenders were not enrolled, and the patents were not delivered. James I. issued a commission to receive the surrenders and re-convey the estates, by new patents, to the lords and gentry, they paying £3,000 for their enrolment in chancery. Though the money was duly paid the enrolment was not made, and the king claimed the land. The titles were pronounced defective, and the whole district was adjudged to vest in the Crown. This unfortunately resulted either from the negligence or wicked design of the officials, based, as Carte observes, " on a mere nicety of law which ought to be tenderly made use of in derogation of the faith and honour of the king's broad seal." The lords and gentry put no faith in the king's sense of equity ; they appealed to his necessities, offered double their annual compositions, and to pay a fine of £10,000. The proposal was entertained, and the western scheme of plantation was suspended.

The jurors were coerced or bribed into finding for the Crown. The judges and law officers were rewarded. Sir Arthur Chichester got large possessions in Ulster, which remain in his family to the present day, his descendant, the Marquis of Donegal, having large estates in Ulster. Sir John Davis was rewarded with a grant of 4,000 acres in the same province. " No means of industry," says Leland, " or devices of craft were left untried, and there are not wanting proofs of the most iniquitous practices of hardened cruelty or vile perjury and scandalous subornation, employed to despoil the fair and unoffending proprietor of his inheritance."

"Where no grant appeared, or descent or conveyance in pursuance of it could be proved (says Carte), the land was immediately adjudged to belong to the Crown. All grants taken from the Crown since 1st Edward II. till 10th Henry VIII. had been resumed by Parliament, and the lands of all absentees, and of all that were driven out by the Irish, were, by various acts, vested again in the Crown. . . . Nor did even later grants afford full security ; for if there was any former grant in being, at the time they were made, or if the patents passed in Ireland were not exactly agreeable to the fiat, and both of these to the king's original warrant transmitted from England—in short, if there was any defect in expressing the tenure, or any mistake in point of form, there was an end of the grant and the estate under it."

The following statutes, confiscating lands in Ireland, were passed :—

Philip and Mary, 3 and 4, cap. i., ii		Disposing of Leix and Offaly.
"	" cap. iii.	Divers and sundry waste grounds into shire grounds.
Elizabeth,	2, cap. vii.	Restitution of the hospital of St. John's.
"	3, cap. iii.	Attainder of Christopher Eustace.
"	11, cap. i.	" of Shane O'Neile.
"	" cap. iii.	" of Thomas, Knight of the Valley.
"	Sep. 4, cap. ii.	Restoring the Earl of Kildare.
"	cap. viii.	Attainder of Sir Oswalde Maasingbred.
"	12, cap. v.	" of all indicted for treason, from April 1, 1569, to April 1, 1571.
"	Sep. 2, cap. v.	" John Fitzgerald, the White Knight.
"	27, cap. i.	" of James Eustace.
"	28, cap. vii.	" of Earl of Desmond.
"	"	" of John Browne and others.

Mr. H. C. Hamilton, F.S.A., Assistant Keeper of the Public Records, in the introduction to the Calendar of State Papers, 1509—1573, says :—

"The power of the English in Ireland had so much decreased in Henry VII.'s time that the old Irish system of government in clans or separate small nations had revived and was in full force throughout the greater part of the land. Of this government and its workings we have the best and most ample accounts in these papers. The wars of Henry VIII., Mary, and Elizabeth, reveal the whole strength and weakness of the system, and show how the superior combination of the English, supported by continual supplies of men and money from home, prevailed over the craft and daring of the native chiefs and favourite generalissimos."

In the arguments in the case of Tanistry, 5th James I., it was alleged "that King John only made twelve counties in Leinster and Munster, viz., Dublin, Meath, Uriel, Kildare, Catherlough, Kilkenny, Wexford, Waterford, Cork, Kerry, Limerick, and Tipperary. But the other provinces and territories of this kingdom, which are now divided into twenty-one counties at large, being then inhabited for the greater part by the mere Irish, were out of the limits of shire ground for the space of 300 years after the making of the first twelve counties, and therefore it was impossible that the common law of England could be executed in these counties and territories: for the law cannot be put in execution where the king's writs cannot run, but where there is a county and a sheriff, or other member of the law, to serve and return the king's writs."

It was further urged "that if a conqueror receives any of the native inhabitants into his protection, and avoweth them for his subjects, and permitteth them to continue their possessions and remain at peace and allegiance, their heirs shall be adjudged in by good title without grant or confirmation of the conqueror." The example of the Norman conquest and that of Wales were instanced as proving the legality of pre-existing customs and rights, and it was urged that James I., by special proclamation in the third year of his reign, declared and published "that he received all the natives of Ireland into his royal protection, by which it was clearly resolved that the common law of England was thereby established universally in the kingdom of Ireland." The common law of England, however, recognises existing customs, and, should have legalized *tanistry*.

English Sovereigns and statesmen appear to have felt that the Irish chieftains who had never held their lands from the Crown, owed it no fealty. Many descendants of English settlers intermarried into Irish families, and adopted the Tanistry system. An effort to substitute holdings under the Crown for the Irish system was made by the xii. Elizabeth, cap. 5; it enables "the pretended lords, gentlemen, and freeholders of the Irishry and degenerated men of English name, holding their land by Irish custom, to surrender their lands to the Queen, and of taking estates by letters patent, which shall be good and effectual in the law, against all persons except those who have estate, title, or right to the said lands by the due course of the common law."

In 1604 Sir Arthur Chichester was appointed deputy, and, Lascelles says,—

"A Commission of GRACE was issued under the great seal of England, empowering the chief governor to accept surrenders of those Irish lords who held of old on precarious tenure. Many embraced this opportunity of converting their tenure for life into one of fee, which should descend to their children. Others dreaded the legal consequences of their late treason, and were impatient to receive their possessions by a new investiture. So that this commission instantly produced a general surrender of lands. No chieftaincies were now granted by letters patent; no officers of justice to be stationed, or to exercise an Irish seigniory. The lord by his new patent was to be invested only with the lands found to be in his immediate possession as a domain. His followers were to be confirmed by the king in their subordinate tenures on condition only of paying the lord the stated rent, in place of all uncertain Irish exactions. Building, planting, cultivation, and civilization were to follow in the train of these regulations. The trading towns were induced to follow the example of the lords; they surrendered their old and accepted new charters with such regulations and privileges as tended to keep them in subjection to the Crown."

"King James I.," says Plowden, pp. 100, 101, "in order more effectually to secure the full dominion both of the Irish and their property, published a proclamation, which is usually called the Commission of Grace, for securing the subjects of Ireland against all claims of the Crown. The chief governor was thereby empowered to accept the surrender of those Irish lords who still held their estates or possessions by the old tenure of *tanistry* or *gavelkind*, and to regrant them in fee simple according to the English law, thus converting the estates for life of the chieftains into estates in fee simple. For this there were two obvious reasons of State policy: the first was that in case of forfeiture the whole would become vested in the Crown by the attainder of the forfeiting person; whereas if by the old tenure of tanistry they remained tenants for life, the estates could only in such cases be forfeited to the Crown for the life of the forfeiting person, and would be saved to all remainder men, which by the old Brehon tenure were in fact the whole sept. The second reason was, that by vesting the fee simple in the chief, which by the course of English law made it descendable to his eldest son or heir-at-law, it excluded the sept from the reversionary distributive rights of gavelkind upon the death of the tenant for life, and thus detached the septs from that common bond of interest and union with their chief which gave them firmness, consistency, and consequence, and necessarily threw them thus disjointed more immediately under the power of the sovereign, by leaving only one freeholder or tenant to the Crown in each sept. The new grants to the lords were limited to the lands in their actual possession, and those lands which any of his followers held on very precarious Irish tenures of the chief were confirmed to the mesne tenant, also in fee, upon paying to the lord a certain rent, equivalent to the lord's beneficial interest in the services or tenure of his tenant. Thus was the whole landed interest of Ireland new modelled, and the example of these new patentees of the Crown was followed by many trading towns and corporations throughout the kingdom: they surrendered their old and accepted new charters from the Crown."

Travelling was difficult in those days, and there was too little disposition to preserve the rights of the inferior holders or ter-tenants. The chieftain went through the ceremony of surrendering the estate of the clan or sept, though he was only joint owner with others, and got a new title to the whole estate. He would not immediately proceed to enforce his new seigniorial rights, and the occupants, finding no change in their treatment, regarded the patent as a confirmation of their existing rights, which entitled them to the possession of the land subject to the payment of tribute. Hence arose the claim for tenant right, which is a continuing assertion of the ancient right of the occupiers. The existence of patents gave the Crown increased rights of forfeiture, and we shall presently see how they were exercised, and in the change of superiors the rights of inferiors were further disregarded, and those who were the real owners of the land were reduced to tenancy or serfdom.

Any proprietary claims by the inferior members of the sept were, however, rudely set aside, not by legislation, but by a resolution of the judges, in regard to which, Professor Sullivan, in the introduction to O'Curry's Lectures, says:—

"In Ireland all the Irish customs were set aside by a judgment given in the year 1605, which more than any other measure, not excepting the repeated confiscations, injured the country, and gave rise to most of the present evils of the Irish land system."

These resolutions are reported by Sir John Davis, and as they are very important I give them *in extenso;* but I cannot find that the case was argued before the court, or that there was either plaintiff or defendant.

Hilary, iii. Jacobi, reported by Sir John Davis,—

"*The resolution of the judges touching the Irish custom of gavelkind.*

"First be it known that the lands possessed by the meer *Irish* within this realm were divided into several territories and countries, and the inhabitants of every Irish county were divided into several septs or lineages.

"Secondly, in every *Irish* territory there was a lord or chieftain, and a *tanist* who was his successor apparent. And of every Irish sept or lineage there was also a chief who was called a canfinny, or *caput cognationis.*

"Thirdly, all the possessions within these Irish territories (before the common law of England was established in this realm as it now is) ran always either in course of *tanistry* or in course of *gavelkind.* Every seigniory or chiefry, with the portion of land which passed with it, went without partition to the *tanist*, who always came in by election or strong hand, and not by descent; but all the inferior tenancies were partible between males in *gavelkind.* Yet the estate which the lord had in his chiefry, or which the inferior tenants had in *gavelkind,* was not an estate of inheritance, but a temporary or transitory possession. For, as the next heir of the lord or chieftain was not to inherit the chiefry, but the oldest and worthiest of the sept (as is shown in the case of *tanistry*), who was often removed and expelled by another who was more active and strong than he, so the lands of the nature of gavelkind were not partible among the next heirs male of him who died seised, but among all the males of his sept, in this manner:—The *canfinny*, or chief of a sept (who was commonly the most ancient of the sept), made all partitions at discretion; and after the death of any ter-tenant, who had a competent portion of land, assembled all the sept, and, having thrown all their possessions into hotchpot, made a new partition of all; in which partition he did not assign to the son of him who had died the portion which his father had, but he allotted to each of the sept, according to his seniority, the better or greater portion. These portions or purparties, being so allotted and assigned, were possessed and enjoyed accordingly, until a new partition was made, which, at the discretion or will of the *canfinny*, was to be made on the death of each inferior tenant, and so, by reason of these frequent transmissions and removals, or translations of the tenants from one portion to another, all the possessions were uncertain; and the uncertainty of the possessions was the very cause that no civil habitations were erected, no enclosure or improvement was made of the land in the Irish countries where the custom of *gavelkind* was in use, especially in Ulster, which seemed to be all one wilderness before the new plantation made by the *English* undertakers there; and this was the fruit of this *Irish gavelkind*."

"Also by this Irish custom of *gavelkind*, bastards had their portions with the legitimate, and wives were utterly excluded of dower, and daughters were not inheritable, although their father had died without issue male. So that this custom differed from the custom of *gavelkind* in Kent, in four points."

"For, 1, by the custom of Kent the land of the nature and tenure of gavelkind is partible among the next heirs, males only; and such co-parceners, after partition, have a certain estate of inheritance in all their portions."

"2. The bastards are not admitted to inherit equally with the legitimate sons."

"3. The wife of every tenant in gavelkind is endowable of a moiety."

"4. In default of males, the heirs female inherit, and therefore the custom of gavelkind used in Kent hath been always allowed and approved of as good and lawful custom by the law of England."

"But this Irish custom of gavelkind was agreeable in several of these points to the custom of gavelkind which was in use in North

Wales, which custom was reproved and reformed by the stat. of Rutland, made 1 & Ed. I. See the stat. of 34 H. VIII., c. 28, where the custom of gavelkind in Wales is utterly abolished, and divers other usages resembling other customs of the Irish."

"For these reasons, and because all the said Irish counties and the inhabitants of them from henceforward were to be governed by the rules of the common law of England, it was resolved and declared by all the judges, that the said Irish custom of gavelkind was void in law, not only for the inconvenience and the unreasonableness of it, but because it was a mere personal custom, and could not alter the descent of inheritance."

"And therefore all the lands in these Irish counties were now adjudged *to descend according to the course of common law*, and that the wives should be endowed, and the daughters should be inheritable to these lands, notwithstanding this Irish custom or usage."

"And where the wives of Irish lords or chieftains claim to have sole property in a certain portion of goods during the coverture, with power to dispose of such goods without the assent of their husbands, it was resolved and declared by all the judges that the property of such goods should be adjudged to be in the husbands and not in the wives, as the common law is in such cases."

This resolution of the judges was, by the special order of the lord deputy, registered amongst the Acts of Council; but then this provision was added to it, "that, if any of the meer Irish had possessed and enjoyed any portion of land by this custom of Irish gavelkind, before the commencement of the reign of our lord the king who now is, he should not be disturbed in his possession, but should be continued and established in it. But that after the commencement of his Majesty's reign all such lands should be adjudged to descend to him by common law, and should be adjudged from henceforward possessed and enjoyed accordingly."

This resolution or decision, fairly carried out, would have given each member of the sept the estate in fee of the land which he held at the commencement of the reign of James I., it would have remained in his family and become an estate of inheritance, thereby effecting in Ireland a change very similar to that which took place in France, Switzerland, and Belgium, whereby the lands owned in common became possessions in severalty, and a class, most useful to the community, who are now called *peasant proprietors*, was created, but this breaking up of the lands in Ireland did not suit the designs of the English adventurers, who wished to have them in large lots, that they might be forfeited and re-granted. It is now almost impossible to trace the means by which the decision of the Council was defeated, but it is apparent that it gave every one of the ter-tenants an estate in fee of the lands in his possession.

It must be borne in mind that America, Australia, and India did not then offer fields for the settlement of English adventurers, while Ireland was looked upon as the almost only place for their migration. The existence of a large number of small estates would not have suited the views of these adventurers, who desired large possessions, and found them more accessible when in few hands.

In 1604 Sir John Davis wrote to Cecil about the state of the Church, and we may judge from it of the anarchy of other holdings:—

"There are ten archbishops, and under them are, or should be, twenty bishops at least. The Churchmen for the most part throughout the kingdom are mere idols and ciphers, and such as cannot read, if they should stand in need of the benefit of their clergy; and yet most of those whereof many be serving men and some horse boys are not without two or three benefices apiece, for the Court of Faculties doth qualify all manner of persons, and dispense with all manner of non-residence and pluralities. For an example of pluralities the Archbishop of Cashel is worthy to be remembered, having now in his hands four bishoprics, Cashel, Waterford, Lismore, and Emly, and threescore and seventeen spiritual livings besides. Should corrupt his lordship too much if he should tell him how they disinherit these churches by long leases, there being no such laws here as in England to restrain them. But what is the effect of these abuses? The churches are ruined and fallen down to the ground in all parts of the kingdom.

There is no divine service, no christening of children, no receiving the sacrament, no Christian meeting or assembly; no, not once in the year: in a word, no more demonstration of religion than amongst Tartars or cannibals."

In another letter to the same statesman he says—

" If justice be well and soundly executed here but for two or three years the kingdom will grow rich and happy, and in good faith he thinks loyal, and will no more, like the lean cow in Pharaoh's dream, devour the fat of the happy realm of England."

A case immediately affecting the question of tanistry was brought before the Court of King's Bench, in Hilary Term, in the 5th of James I. It is reported by Sir John Davis as follows :—

" In Ejectione Firmae, between Murrough MacBryan, plaintiff, and Cahir O'Callaghan (ancestor of Lord Lismore), defendant, on general issue joined, the jury found a special verdict to this effect, viz., that the castle of Dromineen, where the entry and ejectment is supposed to be made, lie within a certain place or precinct of land called Publi-Callaghan, otherwise O'Callaghan's country, within the county of Cork, and time out of mind have been of the tenure and nature of *tanistry;* and that in all lands of the tenure and nature of *tanistry* within Publi-Callaghan aforesaid, such custom hath been used and approved time out of mind, viz., that when any person died seised of any castles, manors, land, or tenements of the nature and tenure aforesaid, then such castles, manors, lands, and tenements ought to descend, and have time out of mind used to descend, *seniori et dignissimo vero sanguinis et cognominis* of such person who so died seised ; and that the daughter or daughters of such person so dying seised, from time out of mind, were not inheritable of such lands or tenements or any part of them.

" The jury further find that Donough MacTeige O'Callaghan, chief of his name, was seised of the seigniory or chieftainship of Publi-Callaghan, and of the lands aforesaid, according to the custom and course of tanistry; and being so seised had issue Conogher O'Callaghan ; Conogher had issue Teige and Eleanor ; Teige had issue Donough MacTeige the younger; Eleanor was married to Arl O'Keeffe ; Conogher and Teige, his son, died in the life of Donough

MacTeige the elder; afterwards the said Donough MacTeige the elder by feoffment, according to the course of common law, executes an estate to Donough MacTeige the younger, and to the heirs male of his body, remainder to the right heirs of the feoffor. Donough MacTeige the elder died, and Donough MacTeige the younger died without issue male; after whose death another Conogher O'Callaghan, being the oldest and most worthy of the blood and surname of O'Callaghan, entered into the land whereto and claimed to hold it as lord and chieftain of Publi-Callaghan, according to the course of tanistry, and was thereof seised *proest lex postulæ*.

"And they further find that the said Conogher being so seised surrendered the said land and all his estate, right, title, and interest in it to Queen Elizabeth; on which the said queen, in consideration of the said surrender, regranted the said land to the said Conogher and his heirs, who entered and enfeoffed one Fagan, who enfeoffed Bryan MacOwen, the lessor of the plaintiff.

"And they lastly find that Arl O'Keeffe and Eleanor his wife died, and after their death Manus O'Keeffe entered and enfeoffed Cahir O'Callaghan, the defendant, who entered and ejected the lessee of Bryan MacOwen, and upon all this matter the jurors pray the advice of the court, &c.

"Upon which one main question ariseth, viz., whether the title of the heir at common law, which the defendant hath, or the title of the *tanist*, which estate the lessor of the plaintiff hath, should be preferred as this case is. And in the discussion of this question three principal points were moved and argued.

"1st. Whether the said custom of tanistry was void or not in itself, or otherwise abolished by the introduction of the common law of England?

"2nd. Admitting that it was a good custom, and not abolished by the common law, whether it be discontinued and destroyed by the feoffment, which created and limited an estate tail in the land, according to the course of the common law, so as that it shall not be reduced to the course of *tanistry*, when the estate tail is determined?

"3rd. Whether Conogher O'Callaghan, who entered as *tanist* after the estate tail determined, gained a better estate by his surrender to Queen Elizabeth and the re-grant made to him by letters patent?"

The arguments in this case were very lengthened and

curious. It depended in the King's Bench for the space of three or four years, and was argued several times, in the course of which the Justices resolved:—

"That as Donough MacTeague held as tanist, which was not an estate in common law, the re-grant by Queen Elizabeth in consideration of the surrender of such estate was void in law, and that Queen Elizabeth shall not be said to be in actual possession of the land by reason of the first conquest, as it did not appear by some reason that the conqueror had appropriated to himself as a parcel of his proper estate, and Sir James Ley, chief justice, had laid down that if the conqueror receiveth any natives into his protection, and avoweth them to be his subjects, and permitteth them to continue their possessions and remain in his peace and allegiance, their heirs shall be adjudged in by good title without grant or confirmation by the conqueror, and shall enjoy their land according to the rules of law which the conqueror hath allowed or established: but afterwards, Sir Humphrey Winch being chief justice, the parties, with leave of the court, came to an agreement by which a reasonable division was made of this territory amongst them; in which division the castle and land in question amongst others were allotted to Cahir O'Callaghan, the defendant; and now, besides their mutual assurance, they have obtained several grants from the king, by virtue of a commission for strengthening defective titles."

The main fact of interest is the finding of the jury that the custom of tanistry had existed time out of mind in this district, and that all the lands had time out of mind descended *seniori et dignissimo vero sanguinis et cognominis* of the person who had died so seised. It was, therefore, a custom at common law, and as such could only be altered or set aside by statute law, and not by a resolution of the Judges.

In 1612 James I. proceeded to the settlement of the O'Neil estate in Ulster, and we have three Acts of Parliament of that year relating to the forfeiture in the north of Ireland; but the most important incident of this reign occurred in the following year, when the flight of Tyrone, and the insurrection of Sir Cahir O'Dogherty, led to the confiscation of their land, amounting to 500,000 acres, in

Donegal, Tyrone, Derry, Fermanagh, Cavan, and Armagh, and enabled James to try his plan of a plantation. Three classes of settlers were encouraged,—undertakers, servitors, and the old inhabitants. The first class was confined solely to the British and Scotch; the second were permitted to take their tenants from Ireland or Britain, provided they were not recusant, and the third were permitted to retain their old religion, and to take the oath of supremacy. The undertakers were entrusted with the places of most strength, the servitors the stations of most danger, and the third class the open country. The properties were to consist of three classes : 1st, 2,000 acres ; 2nd, 1,500 acres ; and 3rd, 1,000 acres ; one-half the escheated lands were to consist of the smallest class, and the other half divided between the two larger classes. Their estates were limited to them and to their heirs. The undertakers got 2,000 acres, which they held of the king *in capite;* the servitors 1,500 acres, which they held by knight's service, and the third 1,000 acres, which were held in common. socage ; all were to reside upon the lands and build upon them. The undertakers were to keep in their own hands a demesne of 600 acres; to have four fee farmers of 120 acres each, six leaseholders of 100 acres each, and on the rest eight families of husbandmen, artificers, and cottagers, and the others lay under like obligations proportionately. No lease was to be less than twenty-one years or three lives. In order to assist the scheme James I. created 200 baronets, who each paid a sum sufficient to maintain thirty men in Ulster for three years at 8d. per day. Such was the general scheme of this plantation. It was found difficult to obtain British tenants. Buildings were slowly erected, the lands were let to the old natives, who offered higher rents, and the conditions of residence were not complied with ; and Sir John Davis, who was attorney-general in this reign, thus speaks of the English system of government :—

" They persuaded the King of England that it was unfit to communicate the laws of England to the Irish, that it was the best policy to hold them as aliens and enemies, and to prosecute them with continual war. Hereby they obtained another royal prerogative and power, which was to make war and peace at their own pleasure, in every part of the kingdom, which gave them an absolute command over the bodies, lands, and goods of the English subjects here."

One of the objects which James I. had in view in the settlement of Ulster, i. e., the formation of an independent yeomanry with perpetuity of tenure, was defeated by the conduct of the patentees, and in 1615 a commission was sent over from England to inquire to what extent the articles which prohibited the undertakers from devising any portion of their lands at will, and enjoined them to make to their tenants certain estates for life, for years, in tail, or in fee simple, at fixed rents, had been observed. Sir Nicholas Pynnar, one of the commissioners, reported that in many cases the articles had been broken and no estates granted by the undertakers. This report was shortly after followed by an information, filed in the Star Chamber A.D. 1637, against the Irish Society and some of the London companies, the result of which was a judgment of forfeiture against the companies because they had not complied with the plantation articles, but let their lands to the highest bidders, without conditions of improvement and without a fixed tenure or a certain rent. The companies, though disregarding the latter of the articles, were forced to treat their tenants according to their spirit, and it was held that, as the company could only grant an estate in perpetuity, the tenant had obtained such an estate, even though there was no deed to prove it, and hence arose the custom of "Ulster Tenant Right," which is a legitimate and legal deduction from the articles granted to the undertakers, who were properly regarded as having granted their tenants that fixity of tenure which they were bound to give. Under this construction of the patents, land held without lease passed from tenant to tenant as if it were assigned by deed, and men acquired the title without lease which the original articles meant them to derive under deeds.

The success of the Ulster plantations encouraged James to attempt the same elsewhere. Sixty-six thousand acres between the rivers Arklow and the Slade, which were for ages possessed by the Irish septs, were found by inquisition to vest in the Crown; and 385,000 acres in Leitrim, Longford, Westmeath, and King's and Queen's Counties. It was found that some parts were possessed anciently by English settlers, who, in the disorders of the kingdom, had been expelled by the natives; other land appeared to be forfeited by rebellion, and these lands, as the lands of absentees, vested in the Crown. Old titles were invalidated: jurors that would not find for the Crown were fined and punished. If the slightest informality were found in the letters patent the lands were seised by the king, who thought thereby to increase his income. In several grants reservations of rent had been made to the Crown, which for ages were not put in force; all such rents were now demanded, or acquittances for the same, and when they were not produced the lands were forfeited.

The following extract from Carte's Life of the Duke of Ormonde, vol. i., pp. 27, 28, will exemplify the manner in which the property of Irish owners was dealt with in the time of James I.:—

"One case in truth was very extraordinary, and contains in it such a scene of iniquity and cruelty that, considered in all its circumstances, it is scarce to be paralleled in the history of any age or any country. *Pheagh MacHugh Byrne*, lord of the *Byrne* territory, now called Ranelagh, in the county Wicklow, being killed in arms towards the latter end of the reign of Queen Elizabeth, she by her letters to Loftus and Gardiner, then lords justices, directed letters patent to be made out for *Phelim MacPheagh*, his eldest son, to have to him and his heirs the county and lands of which his father *Pheagh MacHugh* died seised.

"King James coming to the crown not long after, did in the beginning of his reign give like directions for passing the said inheritance to Phelim, this, *Sir Richard Graham*, an old officer of the army, endeavoured to obstruct, and in order thereto sent out a commission directed to *Sir William Parsons* and others to inquire into the said lands, and upon the inquisition it was found that they were the inheritance of *Pheagh MacHugh Byrne*, father to Phelim, and were then in Phelim MacPheagh's possession. King James, therefore, by a second letter directed that Ranelagh, and all the lands whereof Phelim MacPheagh and Brian his son were then seised should be passed to them and their heirs by letters patent, in consequence whereof another office was taken, in which the lands were found as in the former. The first office was not yet filed, Sir Richard Graham having opposed it, and by his interest and the credit of a general book which he produced, got possession of part of *Phelim's* lands by virtue of a warrant from the Lord Deputy. Sir James Fitz-Piers Fitzgerald attempted likewise to get another part of them passed to him upon the like authority, but Bryan, the son in whose possession they were, complaining at the council-table, Sir James's patent was stayed."

Carte describes the subsequent proceedings, but we must condense the facts. Bryan petitioned the king against Sir Richard Graham, and the case was remitted to the Council Board which examined the matter, and Sir Richard Graham was summoned to England. A commission of four gentlemen were then appointed to examine the matter, and Graham, finding that the final determination was likely to go against him, adopted the expedient of alleging that these lands belonged to the king, and that neither Byrne nor himself had any right. James, always glad to get estates into his possession from defective titles, issued a new commission to Sir William Parsons and others to inquire into the title, Bryan's patron, the Duke of Buckingham, had just gone to Spain, and another patron, the Duke of Richmond, died suddenly, and his enemies, taking advantage of it, Sir William Parsons got the Lord Deputy's warrant to the Sheriff of Wicklow to put Phelim out of the part he enjoyed, and Sir William Parsons and Lord Esmond divided these lands between them. Bryan maintained his right to the lands, and he and his brother were arrested by the conspirators and imprisoned on 13th March, 1625, in Dublin Castle. Informations were sent to two grand juries at Carlow, who did not find the bills, and they were prosecuted in the Star Chamber and fined. The two brothers were kept close prisoners until

20th of August, when Turlogh was enlarged upon parole, and Bryan allowed the liberty of the house. He was set at liberty on Christmas Eve. As they continued their appeal for their lands, a new prosecution was set on foot, and on Nov. 2, 1627, they were sent to Dublin in irons and committed to jail, and Phelim and his five sons were sent to trial at Wicklow. Sir James Fitz-Piers Fitzgerald, an enemy of theirs, and who had part of their estates, though having no property in Wicklow, was foreman. The Lord Chief Justice, upon sight of the evidence, expressed a doubt whether the jury would credit it, upon which Sir Henry Billing pressed him to sign the bill, and said he would undertake that the jury should find it. The jury were the friends or allies of Lord Esmond, Sir William Parsons and others, who had an interest in Byrne's estate, and the grand jury found the bill. The friends of the persecuted gentlemen petitioned the king, and a commission was sent over to inquire into the affair, which consisted of the Lord Primate, the Lord Chancellor, the Archbishop of Dublin, the Lord Chief Justice, and Sir Arthur Savage. It sat in November and December, 1628. When the foul conspiracy against the Byrnes was made apparent they were restored to their liberty, though not to their estate, a considerable part having, during their imprisonment, passed to Sir William Parsons, under letters patent, dated the 4th of August, 4 Car. I.

When James ascended the throne of England, Lord Bacon addressed him in the following language:—" You have found what Ireland barbarous has proved; beware of Ireland civilized." The policy he inaugurated was adapted to retard or prevent the civilization of Ireland. His deputies and representatives, greedy for the possessions of the people, lashed them into rebellion, and then seized upon their land because they resisted. They thus became possessed of the land of the oppressed.

The example set by James and his deputy, Chichester, was followed in the reign of his unfortunate son, and by his able but unscrupulous ministers. Charles I. not having the

means of paying his troops, and being anxious to increase
their number, caused them to be quartered on several
counties and towns in Ireland, the inhabitants of which were
expected to supply them with clothes, provisions, and other
necessaries for three months at each place in turn. Lord
Falkland, the deputy, recommended a cheerful submission,
and promised that *graces* should be granted by his Majesty as
a compensation. The principal nobility and gentry assembled,
and offered a contribution of £40,000 a year for three years,
on certain terms, among which the subjects were secured in
the possession of their lands by a limitation of the king's
title to sixty antecedent years, and a renunciation of all claims
of an earlier period. The inhabitants of Connaught were
admitted to secure their titles from future litigation by a
new enrolment of their patents, and a parliament was to be
summoned for a confirmation of their several estates to all
the proprietors and their heirs.

Charles accepted the money, but he trifled with the latter
condition; Lord Falkland, who made the promise, was
recalled, and Wentworth was appointed. Soon after his arrival
in Ireland he determined to subvert the title of every estate
in Connaught, which had been principally granted by the
commission of defective titles in the previous reign. He
ordered inquisitions as to title to take place in each county
in that province, and attended these inquisitions, accompanied
by a force sufficient to overawe the jurors. Those of Roscommon and Leitrim were so much intimidated that they
found for the Crown; those of Mayo and Sligo followed the
example. The jurors of Galway were privately encouraged
by Ulric de Burgo, Earl of Clanricarde, who was a favourite
with Charles and resided at the English court, to resist the
designs of the lord deputy, and at the inquisition in 1635
they found the following curious verdict :—" That the acquisition of Connaught by Henry II. was not a conquest, but a
submission of the inhabitants; and that the grant of Roderic
was barely a composition, whereby the king had only
dominion, and not the property in the land." The lord

F

deputy was enraged at this decision, he fined the sheriff
£1,000 for summoning such jurors, and bound them to
appear to answer for their offence in the Castle Chamber,
Dublin, where each of them was fined £4,000, and sentenced
to imprisonment until the fine was paid. Some of them
died in prison. A fresh inquisition was held, when the
jurors were more submissive, and found for the Crown.
Ulric de Burgo used his influence to procure the release of
the obstinate jurors, and some of them were set at liberty.
The lord deputy's scheme of plantation was abandoned,
and the inhabitants were confirmed in their property.

The litigation which ensued upon the schemes of Wentworth led to a remarkable trial, and subsequently to the publication of Sir Henry Spelman's treatise on feuds. The case affected the property of Lord Dilton, and in the preface to Spelman on feuds it is thus described:—

"The several manors and estates within the counties Roscommon, Sligo, Mayo, and Galway, in the kingdom of Ireland, being unsettled as to their titles, King James I., by commission dated 2nd March, in the fourth year of his reign, did authorize certain commissioners by letters patent to make grants of the said lands and manors to their respective owners, whereupon several letters patent to that effect passed under his Majesty's Great Seal by virtue of the said commission for the strengthening of titles that might otherwise seem defective. And afterwards, in the reign of King Charles I., upon an inquiry into his Majesty's title to the county of Mayo, there was an Act of State published commanding all those who held any land by letters patent from the Crown to produce them for enrolment thereof before the Lord Deputy and Council by a certain day, to the end that they might be secured in the quiet possession of their estates, in case the said letters were allowed by that board to be good and effectual in law.

"In pursuance of this order, several letters patent were produced, and particularly the Lord Viscount Dillon's, which, upon the perusal and consideration thereof by his Majesty's Council, were thought to be void in law, and therefore it was ordered by the Lord Deputy and Council that the doubt arising upon the letters patent should be drawn into a case, and that case should be openly argued in the

Council Board. The case was drawn up in these words: 'King James, by commission under the Great Seal, dated the 2nd day of March, in the fourth year of his reign, did authorise certain commissioners to grant the manor of Dale, by letters patent under the Great Seal of this kingdom, to A. and his heirs, and there is no duration given in the said commission touching the tenure to be reserved. There are letters patent by colour of the said commission passed unto A. and his heirs to hold by knight's service as of his Majesty's castle in Dublin. It was asked whether the deficiency of the tenure did so far affect the grant as wholly to destroy the letters patent, or whether the letters patent might be good as to the land, and void only as to the tenure? The question was argued several days in the year 1637, and the court had to inquire what the reservation of tenure is to the grant? whether it be a part of the grant and the *modus concessionis*, or whether it be a distinct thing and *aliud* from the grant? For,' it was said, 'if the reservation of the tenure and the grant of the land be *aliud* and aliened, two distinct things in the consideration of the whole grant made, and the authority given by the commission for the making thereof, then the patent may be void as to tenure, and yet good for the grant of the land. But if the reservation of the tenure be incident unto the authority and included within it, and the reservation of the tenure and the grant of the land make up but one entire grant, so that the one is part of the other, and the reservation of the tenure be *modus concessionis*, then the granting of the land reserving a diverse or contrary tenure to that which their (nude) authority did warrant them to reserve in doing of *idem alio modo*, and so the whole act is void.'"

Those who pleaded for the validity of the letters patent as to the lands, and their being void only as to tenure, urged among other arguments that tenure *in capite* was brought into England by the Conquest, but grants were by common law, and therefore grants being more ancient than tenure, the tenure must of necessity be *aliud* from the thing granted.

This led the court to a consideration of the question as to Saxon tenures:—

"It was argued that those called *Thanis Majores* or *Thanis Regis* were the king's immediate tenants of lands which they held by personal service, as of the king's person by grand seigniority or knight's service *in capite*. The land so held was, it was said, in those times called *Thaneland*, as land holden in socage was called *Reveland* so frequently in the Doomsday Book. After the Norman conquest the title of *Thane* and *Thaneland* gave place to *Baron* and *Barony*, and the possessions of the abbots and bishops, which under the Saxons were free from all secular services, were made subject to knight's service *in capite*, but these possessions were converted into baronies, while thanelands were held by that tenure as before. The king's thane was a tenant *in capite*, and the middle thane a tenant by knight's service. It was contended also that reliefs for earls and thanes were in existence and proved by the laws of Edward the Confessor; that wardships were also in use both in England and Scotland before the Norman conquest. The judges, therefore, after full argument, held that feudal tenures existed in England before the Norman conquest."

As this contradicted the assertions made by Sir Henry Spelman in his Glossary, wherein he described feuds as having come into use with the Conquest. It led him into a fuller examination of the question, and to his writing his celebrated treatise upon Feuds.

The question raised in Lord Dillon's case was,—

"Whether the said letters patent be void on the whole or only as to the tenure."

The case was argued on several days, first by Nicholas Plunket for Lord Dillon, and Serjeant Catlor for the king, and because it was a case of great weight and importance it was delivered unto the judges, and they were required by the Lord Deputy and Council to consider it, and to return their resolution touching it; but they not agreeing in opinion, it was thought necessary for public satisfaction that it should be argued solemnly by them all; and consequently, in Trinity Term, the case was argued before the judges, who held by a majority of *five* to *two*,—

"1. That the commissioners by the commission (the Commission of Grace) have a good and legal and sufficient power and authority to grant.

"2. That all letters patent made upon this commission in which they have pursued their authority are good and effectual in law where they have either reserved an express tenure by knight's service *in capite*, or no tenure, for then the law implies a tenure *in capite*.

"3. But where the commissioners reserve a mean tenure the whole patent is void."

They give seven grounds for this decision, being principally that they have exceeded their authority. For these reasons they did resolve—

"That this express reservation (knight's service) of a mean tenure tends to the destruction of the whole patent, and makes it void in law, both as to the lands and to the tenure."

The council board on the 13th July, 1637, issued a proclamation declaring the said letters patent to be wholly void in law, and disallowing all such letters patent for any lands, tenements, or hereditaments in any of the counties Roscommon, Sligo, Galway, or the county of the town of Galway.

These proceedings naturally created wide-spread disaffection. A parliament was convened in 1634, but great care was taken in the nomination of the sheriffs, and in the procuring of the return of Government candidates. Wentworth then succeeded in voting the supplies, but he prevented the passing of the *graces*, and he further succeeded in inducing them to assure the king that he was not bound, either in justice, honour, or conscience, to perform the solemn promise he had made. His theory was that the king's Irish subjects had forfeited the rights of men and citizens. An ancient State paper, which describes the heads of the causes which moved the Irish to take arms in 1641, says, "Many of the natives were expelled out of their possessions, and as many hanged by martial law without any cause and against the law of the realm, and many destroyed and made away with by sinister means and practices."

The parliament from which so much was expected was

prorogued without passing the bills, and the hopes of the king's Irish subjects were extinguished. Their earnest respectful remonstrances had been continuously spurned, and they were driven to desperation. "Half the realm was found to belong to his Majesty, as his ancient demesnes and inheritance, upon old, feigned titles of 300 years past by juries against law, their evidence, and conscience, who were corrupted to find the said titles, upon promise of part of the lands so found for the king or other rewards ; or else drawn thereto by threats of the judges in the circuit, or heavy fines, mulcts, and censures of pillory, sty-marking, and other cruel and unusual punishments."

The banner of revolt was hoisted : the people of Ulster, driven from their homes to starve in woods and forests, swept like a torrent over the plains which once belonged to them, and in one week O'Neil was at the head of 30,000 men. The lords and gentlemen of the Pale, who were mostly of English descent, repaired in great numbers to Dublin, and applied to the Government for arms and authority to array themselves on the side of the Crown, but their application was insultingly refused, and they were ordered by proclamation bearing date October 28, 1641, to leave Dublin within twenty-four hours. They were forced into revolt. The Lords Justices Borlase and Parsons justified their conduct by declaring, "The more rebels, the more confiscation." Extensive forfeitures were the principal object of the chief governors and their friends. "Whatever were their professions, the only danger they really apprehended was that of a speedy suppression of the rebels." Troops arrived from England and Scotland. The English Parliament, with the reluctant consent of the king, passed an Act (the Act of Subscription of Charles I.) reserving 2,500,000 acres of arable meadow and pasture land in Ireland, out of 10,000,000 assumed to have been already forfeited by the insurgents ; as security for money advanced in England for the expenses of the war. The orders of the lords in council to the army were "to wound, kill, slay, and destroy all the rebels and their adherents and relievers and burn, spoil, waste, consume, and destroy, and demolish all places, towns, and houses where the rebels were or have been relieved or harboured, and all the corn and hay there, and to kill and destroy all the men there inhabiting able to bear arms." In the execution of these orders the Lords Justices declare that the soldiers murdered all persons promiscuously, not sparing the women, and sometimes not the children.

The downfall of Stafford led to the appointment of a committee of the Irish Lords and Commons, who demanded the *graces* as a settlement of the land question. The delay of Charles in acceding to their wishes alienated them from the monarch, and the committee entered into correspondence with the leaders of the disaffected portion of the English Parliament. The Marquis of Ormonde was appointed Lord Deputy, and became leader of the Irish royalists, who adhered to the cause of Charles with greater fidelity than could have been expected from their previous ill-treatment. Yet the mass of the Irish people who had been deprived of their possessions by the displacement of the tanistry system of landholding were disaffected to the royal cause. A large section of them, guided by the advice of the papal nuncio, refused a hearty co-operation, and this naturally embarrassed the king's forces. Ormonde held most of the fortified places in Ireland; Dublin, Derry, and Belfast were the only strongholds of the Parliament. The success of Ormonde induced the Parliament to appoint Cromwell Lord Deputy, and he was accompanied to Ireland by a considerable army. He completely broke the power of the royalists. The sack of Drogheda was a fearful exhibition of his power; he showed no mercy. Other fortresses were captured, the garrisons were put to the sword, and whole cities were left unpeopled.

Cromwell's success was followed by the expatriation of 30,000 to 40,000 able-bodied men, who might have been very troublesome had they remained at home. They entered the service of foreign states, and formed the celebrated Irish Brigade, which was recruited by a further expatriation in the reign of William III. The gallant conduct of the Irish at the battle of Dettingen led George III. to exclaim, "Accursed be the laws which have deprived me of such subjects!" Cromwell forced the families of those who had entered foreign service on board ship, and carried them to the West Indies. The numbers are variously estimated at from 6,000 to 100,000. Four Parliamentary Commissioners were named to govern Ireland. Their courts were called "Cromwell's slaughterhouses." The cry was for blood, and they came as sheep to the slaughter. The next act was to banish all "*the Irish*" into Connaught and Clare. The object was to leave the other three provinces to English and Scotch settlers. The design being to obtain the land by the first Act of Settlement, the forfeiture of two-thirds of their estates had been pronounced against those who had borne arms against the Parliament of England or their forces, and one-third against those who had resided in Ireland any time from Oct. 1, 1649, to Nov. 1, 1650, and had not been in the actual service of Parliament, or supported its interests. By the second Act of Settlement it was provided that all persons claiming under the former qualification should get not a portion of their land, but an equal area at the west of the Shannon in Connaught or Clare.

These vast appropriations enabled that ambitious soldier to disband an army of which he was afraid; to remove from England the extreme Puritans, who might have been unruly, and to divert their attention from his policy to that of those whom they displaced. The land seized upon, provided a fund from which he was able to discharge their arrears of pay without raising taxes, which might prove obnoxious. The animosity which first showed itself against the queen of Charles I. found ample vent in Ireland against her co-religionists. Cromwell issued in 1652 debentures in the following form:—

"All lawful deductions made, there remaineth due from the Commonwealth to   , his executors, administrators, and assigns, until the date hereof, the sum of   , which sum is to be satisfied out of the rebels' lands, houses, tenements, and hereditaments in Ireland, in the disposal of the Commonwealth of England.

"Dated the   day of   165—."

These debentures bear upon their face a falsehood; the Irish were not rebels against the English Parliament. They had not forfeited their lands by rebellion, inasmuch as they owed it no allegiance. To carry out the iniquitous designs of the regicides, it was necessary that they should get rid of their own army. They lacked the means of payment, and provided it out of the lands of the Irish. Courts were established in Dublin and Athlone for the determining of claims which should be made; a limited time only was allowed. Four Commissioners of Parliament were sent over,—Edmund Ludlow, Miles Corbet, John Jones, and John Weaver. The Irish were driven across the Shannon, and confined within its limits by a chain of garrisons. The adventurers accepted as a full satisfaction the moiety of the forfeited lands in nine principal counties. A revenue was reserved for disabled soldiers, and for the widows and orphans of those who had fallen in the parliamentary service (except a part of the lands of bishops, and of deans and chapters, granted to the University of Dublin); these, with the forfeited lands in the counties of Dublin, Kildare, Carlow, and Cork, remained unappropriated, and were reserved by Parliament for future disposal. In 1653 the debentures were sold freely and openly for 4s. and 5s. per pound; and 20s. of debentures, one place with another, did purchase two acres of land, at which rate all the land of Ireland, estimated at 8,000,000 of profitable acres, might have been had for £1,000,000, which in 1641 had been worth above £8,000,000.

Dr. (afterwards Sir William) Petty arrived in Waterford in 1652 as physician to the army in Ireland. On the 11th of December, 1654, he obtained a contract from the Government for admeasuring the forfeited lands intended for Cromwell's soldiers at the rate of £7 3s. 4d. per 1,000 acres. By this contract he gained £9,000, and he afterwards got £900 more for a survey of the adventurers' lands. Through these means and his private savings he realized about £13,000, with which sum he bought up soldiers' debentures, and acquired large portions of forfeited lands intended for them. When subsequently accused of having obtained his vast estates through undue influences, he defended himself by explaining, as he afterwards stated in his will, that he had "raised about £13,000 in ready money at a time when, without art, interest, or authority, men bought as much land for 10s. in real money as in this year, 1685, yields 10s. per annum above quit rents."

To such an extent was the removal of the people of some districts carried, that Sir William Petty states,—

"The people of Tipperary have more universally obeyed the order of transportation than other counties generally had done; that county became so uninhabited and waste that it was impossible to find means to do the work tolerably well."

An order which was made in the Privy Council during the Protectorate proves the extent of the depopulation. It runs thus:—

"Whereas Mr. Henry Pain, late one of the Commissioners of Revenue at Clonmel, hath informed us that the transplantation hath been so effectually carried on in the county of Tipperary, and especially in the barony of Eliogarty, that no inhabitant of the Irish nation that knows the country is left in the barony, which may be a great prejudice to the Commonwealth, for want of information of the bounds of the respective territories and the lands therein upon admeasurement; it is therefore ordered that it be referred to the Commissioners of Loughrea to consider if four fit and knowing persons of the Irish nation, lately removed out of the barony into Connaught, and to return them with their families to reside in or near their old habitations, for the due information of the surveyors appointed of the respective bounds of each parcel of land admeasurable, and to continue there until further order.

"Dublin, 20 December, 1654.

"THOMAS HERBERT,
" Clerk of the Council."

An almost complete transplantation of the people of

Tipperary into Connaught took place. The new settlers were not secure as to their title, and many of them obtained forced conveyances and re-leases from the former proprietors. Clarendon, in his life, says,—

"What should they do? They could not be permitted to go out of this precinct to shift for themselves elsewhere; and without their assignment in Connaught they must starve there as many did die every day of the famine. In this deplorable condition and under this consternation they found themselves obliged to accept or submit to the hardest conditions, and so signed such conveyances and re-leases as were prepared for them."

The war of extermination was carried to such a fearful extent that it was made lawful for any of the English settlers to kill any Irish person, man, woman, or child, that was found east of the Shannon, and the common expression of these murderers towards their victims was, "To hell or Connaught with you!" Humanity recoils and shudders at the fearful atrocities which were committed, and history has no blacker page than that which records the sufferings inflicted upon the Irish during the Protectorate.

Under these circumstances the population of Ireland very seriously diminished. Sir William Petty estimated the loss of population between 1641 and 1682 at 504,000, and Clarendon tells us,—

"That there was a large tract of land even to the half of the province of Connaught that was separated from the rest of Ireland by a long and large moor, and which by plague and many massacres remained almost desolate; into this space and circuit of land they required the Irish to retire by such a day, under the penalty of death, and all who should after that time be found in any part of the kingdom, man, woman, or child, should be killed by anybody who saw or met them."

Sir William Petty, in 1672, estimated the population of Ireland at about a million one hundred thousand persons.

Colonel Lawrence, an eye-witness, writes :—

"About the year 1652-1653, the plague and famine had so

swept away whole countries that a man might travel twenty or thirty miles without seeing a living creature, either man, beast, or bird, they being all dead or having quitted the desolate places. Our soldiers would tell stories of where they saw a smoke by day or fire or candle by night, and when we did meet with two or three poor cabins, none but very aged men, women, and children (and those with the prophet might have complained, 'We are become as a bottle in the smoke, our skin is black as an oven' because of the terrible famine) were found in them."

The restoration of Charles II. was seized upon by his supporters as the signal for resuming their estates; those who had been deprived of their lands returned and repossessed themselves of their patrimonies by force even before the king was proclaimed. This rashness was represented as a new rebellion, and the Cromwellian settlers, alarmed for their possessions, procured an Act of indemnity before the king landed, which excluded all those who thus tried to regain their lands. It was so worded as to amount to the exclusion of the whole of the Roman Catholic party. On the king's arrival in London he issued a proclamation commanding the continuance of undisturbed possession to adventurers and soldiers of all manors, houses, and lands as they then held until legally invested, or his Majesty, with the advice of Parliament, should take further measures in these affairs. At length, after much delay, on a calculation formed by the Earl of Orrery, Sir John Clotworthy, and Sir Arthur Mervyn, it was found that, besides the land possessed by the soldiers, enough remained to compensate all the innocent or meritorious Irish, and Charles published his famous declaration for the settlement of the kingdom.

By this declaration the adventurers were to be confirmed in the lands possessed by them on the 7th May, 1659, according to the Acts made in the previous reign, which they were to hold in fee and common socage, and all deficiencies were to be satisfied before May, 1660. With the exception of ecclesiastical lands and some other provisoes, the soldiers were confirmed in the lands allotted for their pay, which they were to hold by knights' service *in capite;* officers who had served before June, 1649, were to receive 12s. 6d. in the pound by estates and other securities. Protestants, unless they had been in rebellion or had taken decrees for land in Connaught or Clare, were to be restored to their lands. Innocent Catholics were restored to their estates, and Catholics who submitted and adhered to the peace of 1648 were to be restored to their ancient properties upon the reprisal of those who held them. This declaration of settlement gave little satisfaction to any party. The Royalist officers received but little more than half their pay, and the ancient landholders, who had suffered for the royal cause and were in a state of poverty, were excluded from their estates until they could repay those who had been quartered upon them by Cromwell. The commissioners appointed to carry the declaration of settlement into effect were partial to the soldiers and adventurers, and threw much difficulty in the way of the Catholic proprietors, who tried to establish their innocence. The Parliament which was convened in 1661 to confirm the Act of Settlement was mainly elected by those in illegal possession of the estates. It tried by statute to exclude the Catholics, many of whom claimed their property from Parliament. An inquiry was instituted by the House of Lords, which revealed many malpractices by the commissioners. Widows were deprived of their jointures, orders of the king for the restitution of particular persons were eluded; the Lords resolved to address the king to revoke the illegal grants made by the commissioners, and a deputation waited on Charles in London claiming redress.

The Irish Cromwellians accepted the restoration without much difficulty, but they kept a firm grasp on their lands. After a long struggle of controversy, bribery, and intrigue on the part of the claimants, and wavering and irresolution on the part of the Government, the Puritans carried the day and kept their lands. The Acts of Settlement and explanation which closed the question of proprietorship, have been called the great charter of this party, they decided the title to the lands; yet, for many years after this time, a great part of the land of Ireland continued to be held by forcible and disputed possession.

Petty's Political Anatomy of Ireland contains the following information relating to this period :—

Area of Ireland		10,500,000 acres.
Rivers, loughs, &c.	1,500,000	
Unprofitable land	1,500,000	
Arable and pasture	7,500,000	
		10,500,000 ,,
1641. Belonging to Papists and sequestered Protestants	5,200,000	
To the Church	300,000	
Protestants planted by Elizabeth and James	2,000,000	
		7,500,000 ,,
Restored to twenty-six who proved of good affection	40,000	
The Duke of Ormonde	130,000	
Lord Inchiqun, Lord Roscommon, &c.	40,000	
	210,000	

Innocent Papists	1,200,000	
The Church	20,000	
Duke of York	120,000	
		1,340,000
To Letterers & Innocent Irishmen	60,000	
To Papists per proviso Colkin	360,000	
		420,000
Left in the common stock	80,000	
To adventurers	390,000	
		470,000
Soldiers seised		1,440,000
To forty-nine officers	280,000	
To Protestants per proviso	270,000	
		550,000
Upon transplantation decrees	700,000	
Restored to mortgagees	100,000	
	800,000	
		5,200,000 ,,

Of lands seised by usurpers the Papists have recovered	2,340,000	
New Protestants and churches additional	2,400,000	
Of a more indifferent nature	460,000	
		5,200,000 ,,

7,500,000 acres good
1,500,000 „ coarse

9,000,000 acres, worth		£900,000
Quit and Crown rents . . .	£ 90,000	
Tithes	162,000	
Benefit of leases and tenants' improvements	216,000	
Landlords	432,000	
		£900,000

He divides :—

The landlords' share of this . . .	£432,000	
2,520,000 acres gained by the Rebellion	£144,000	
Adventurers and soldiers . .	108,000	
Soldiers alone	86,400	
The King gained :—	£338,400	
Augmented the Church, the Duke of York and others .		£770,000
Paid adventurers and officers		670,000
Gained on usual revenue of above . . .		80,000
Or at fifteen years' purchase		1,200,000
Gained the year's value, &c., worth		300,000

Freed himself of the articles with the Irish of 1648.

Population :—Papists . .	800,000	} 1,100,000	
Non-Papists .	300,000		
English . .	200,000		
Scots . .	100,000		
Irish . .	800,000	1,100,000	
		2,200,000	

Houses :— 160,000 without chimneys

24,000, 1 chimney, at £5 . .				£120,000
6,800, 2 to 3 chimneys, at £	40			272,000
5,600, 4 „ 6 „ „	100			560,000
2,500, 7 „ 9 „ „	300			750,000
700, 10 „ 12 „ „	600			420,000
400, 13 „ 20 „ „	1,000			400,000
20 transcendental houses .				78,000
				£2,600,000

Cattle, 6,000,000, or equivalents in horses and sheep .	3,000,000
Exports from Ireland	£500,000
Absentees' rents, &c.	£200,000
Cattle exports	140,000
The whole substance of Ireland was worth . . .	£16,000,000
The customs revenue exceeded	£32,000

The defeat of James II. and his flight from Ireland led to a reversal of his policy, but his troops, after a gallant contest with the veterans of William III., made terms with him. The Treaty of Limerick, which should have formed the basis of future legislation, contained a provision that the Irish should enjoy the same privilege in the exercise of religion as they had done in the reign of Charles II., and that they should be reinstated in their properties, real and personal, and in all their rights, titles, and privileges, on taking the oath of allegiance to King William. The Irish Parliament of 1695 annulled the Act of James II., and confirmed and explained the Act of Settlement. Large forfeitures were made, and William, who, from the insufficiency of the parliamentary supplies, was unable to reward his dependants, adopted the Cromwellian plan, and made seventy-six grants out of the Irish forfeited estates. Eight of these grants were as follows :—

135,820	acres to	Lord Woodstock (van Bentinck).
108,633	„	Earl of Albemarle (van Keppel).
95,649	„	Countess of Orkney (Miss Eliz. Villiers).
49,517	„	Lord Romney (Sidney).
39,871	„	Earl of Rochford (de Zuleistan).
36,148	„	Earl of Galway (de Ravigney).
30,512	„	Marquis de Pursai.
26,480	„	Earl of Athlone (de Ginkel).
522,630		

The Parliament were offended at this Act of Prerogative, and the English Commons charged the king with a breach of promise in not having left the forfeitures to the disposal of Parliament for the discharge of the public debts. It passed an Act for sending seven commissioners to inquire into the value of the confiscated estates, and the reason of their alienation, and upon the report of these commissioners, "The Act of Resumption" (11 & 12 Will. III., c. 2, Engl.) was passed, A.D. 1700; it voided all royal grants of land made after the 13th February, 1788, and directed an absolute sale

of all Irish estates which had belonged to James II. or his
adherents. The English Commons were so aware of the
violence of their act that they voted, contrary to constitutional
rights, that no petition should be recorded against it. Yet
petitions were sent in large numbers, and the trustees were
charged with injustice and venality. The granted lands,
which were valued at £1,500,000, hardly realized one-third of
that sum.

A more recent authority, who can hardly be accused of
partiality to the Irish—Lord Chancellor Fitzgibbon (Earl of
Clare)—in a speech made in 1799, said,—

"After the expulsion of James II. from the throne of England, the
old inhabitants made a final effort for the recovery of their ancient
power, in which they were once more defeated by an English army,
and the slender relics of Irish possession became the subject of fresh
confiscation. From the report made by the commissioners appointed
by the Parliament of England in 1698, it appears that the Irish
subjects outlawed for the rebellion of 1688 amounted to 3,978, and
that their Irish possessions, as far as could be computed, were of the
value of £210,623, comprising 1,670,792 acres. This fund was sold,
under the authority of an English Act of Parliament, to defray the
expenses incurred by England in reducing the rebels of 1688, and the
sale introduced into Ireland a new set of adventurers. It is a very
curious and important speculation to look back to the forfeitures of
Ireland incurred in the last century. The superficial contents of the
island are calculated at 11,042,682 acres. Let us now examine the
state of the forfeitures.

In the reign of James I. the whole of the province
of Ulster was confiscated, containing . 2,836,837 acres.
Let out by the Court of Claims at the Restoration 7,800,000 „
Forfeitures of 1688 . . . . . 1,060,792 „

Total . . . 11,697,629 „

So that the whole of your island has been confiscated, with the
exception of the estates of four or six families of English blood, some
of whom had been attainted in the reign of Henry VIII., but
recovered their possessions before Tyrone's rebellion, and had the
good fortune to escape the pillage of the English republic inflicted

by Cromwell; and no inconsiderable portion of the island has been confiscated twice or perhaps thrice in the course of a century. The situation, therefore, of the Irish nation at the Revolution stands unparalleled in the history of the inhabited world. If the wars of England carried on here from the reign of Elizabeth had been waged against a foreign enemy, the inhabitants would have retained their possessions under the established law of civilized nations, and their country have been annexed as a province to the British Empire."

Some of the laws affecting land were most injurious; that, for example, which enacted that no Papist should have a horse of greater value than £5, so deteriorated the breed of horses that an enactment, 8 Anne, c. iii., s. 34, was passed as follows:—

"And whereas by the laws of this land Papists are not qualified to keep any horse, mare, or gelding of above £5 value, which has been found prejudicial so far forth as the same relates to stud mares, be it enacted that no stud mare kept for breeding only, nor stallion kept as such, and for no other use, shall be deemed or taken to be within the intention of the Act entitled, 'An Act for better securing the Government by disarming the Papists,' but that every Papist, and reputed Papist, may keep such stud mares and stallions notwithstanding the said Act, or any law to the contrary, and the breed or produce thereof under the age of five years, and not otherwise."

The law which prevented "Papists" having any greater tenure than thirty years, where the rent reserved was less than two-thirds of the value, was calculated to prevent any improvement in their condition or in the system of agriculture. This policy was the result of the abnormal relations of two classes—the plunderers and the plundered, the owner and the occupier. The former, possessed of political power and supported by the armies of England, enacted oppressive and restrictive laws; the statute-book and the concurrent testimony of all authorities prove that it was their stern resolve that the mass of the people should be denied all interest in the lands which they cultivated, and be condemned to live on the coarsest food, and reside in habitations unfit for human beings, while the utmost rent was wrung from them. Dean Swift, writing in 1729, says,—

" Upon determination of all leases made before the year 1690, a gentleman thinks he has but indifferently improved his estate if he has only doubled his rent roll. Leases are granted but for a small term of years, tenants are tied down to harsh conditions, and discouraged from cultivating the land they occupy to the best advantage by the certainty they have of the rent being raised on the expiration of their leases, proportionate to the improvements they shall make. Thus it is that honest industry is depressed, and the farmer is a slave to the landlord."

The complaint made by Dean Swift is in effect that the labour or the representative of the labour of the tenant became without any compensation the property of the landlord, and that he who expended his labour and capital upon the land was compelled to pay another man for the property which he by his industry and labour had created.

I shall conclude the history of this period, and the description of the effects of these laws, with the following extract from the writings of Edmund Burke:—

" The laws," says he, " have disabled three-fourths of the inhabitants of Ireland from acquiring any estate of inheritance for life, or for years, or any charge whatsoever on which two-thirds of the improved yearly value is not reserved for thirty years. This confinement of landed property to one set of hands, and preventing its free circulation through the community, is a most leading article of ill policy; because it is one of the most capital discouragements to all industry which may be employed on the lasting improvement of the soil, or in any way conversant about land. A tenure of thirty years is evidently no tenure upon which to build, to plant, to raise enclosures, to change the nature of the ground, to make any new experiment which might improve agriculture, or to do anything more than what may answer the immediate and momentary calls of rent to the landlord, and leave subsistence to the tenant and his family. Confine a man to momentary possession, and you at once cut off that laudable avarice which every wise state has cherished as one of the first principles of its greatness. Allow a man but a temporary possession, lay it down as a maxim that he never can have any other, and you immediately and infallibly turn him to temporary enjoyments; and these enjoyments are never the pleasures of labour and free industry, and whose quality it is to famish the present hours and squander all upon prospect and futurity; they are, on the contrary, those of a thoughtless, loitering, and dissipated life. The people must be inevitably disposed to such pernicious habits merely from the short duration of their tenure which the law has allowed. But it is not enough that industry is checked by the confinement of its views, it is further discouraged by the limitation of its own direct object, profit. This is a regulation extremely worthy of our attention, as it is not a consequential, but a direct discouragement to amelioration, as directly as if the law had said in direct terms, 'Thou shalt not improve.' But we have an additional argument to demonstrate the ill policy of denying the occupiers of land any solid property in it. Ireland is a country wholly unplanted. The farms have neither dwelling-houses nor good offices; nor are the lands, almost anywhere, provided with fences and communications; in a word, in a very unimproved state. The landowner there never takes upon him, as is usual in this kingdom, to supply all these conveniences, and to set down his tenant in what may be called a completely furnished farm. If the tenant will not do it, it is never done. This circumstance shows how miserably and peculiarly impolitic it has been in Ireland to tie down the body of the tenantry to short and unprofitable tenures. A finished and furnished house will be taken for any tenure, however short; if the repair lies on the owner, the shorter the better. But no one will take one, not only unfurnished, but half built, but upon a term which on calculation will answer with profit all his charges. It is on this principle that the Romans established their *Emphyteosis*, or fee farm; for although they extended the ordinary term of location only to nine years, yet they encouraged a more permanent letting to farms, with the condition of improvement, as well as annual payment on the part of the tenant, where the land had been rough and neglected; and therefore invented this species of ingrafted holding in the latter times, when property came to be worse distributed by falling into a few hands."

The laws to which Mr. Burke referred in this passage were those which were enacted in the reign of the last of the Stuart monarchs. The first of this race abolished the tanistry system, which gave each man a life interest in a certain portion of the soil, and so forfeited large districts. His successors followed in the path of spoliation; a new class of owners came into possession, whose laws prevented the improvement of the land, and thus lessened the supply of food, and diminished the population. The tide of confiscation ebbed and flowed during these reigns, but in so doing the native possessors were almost entirely swept away.

V.—THE HANOVERIAN PERIOD.

"The evil that men do lives after them."

THE history of the period that elapsed between the death of Queen Anne and the accession of Queen Victoria is an illustration of the truth of the sapient exclamation of the bard of Avon. "The settlement" commenced by the first Stuart sovereign, and carried out so ruthlessly down to the close of the last reign of that dynasty, originated in a wish to extend the royal prerogative and increase the regal revenue. The scheme of Ahab to possess the vineyard of Naboth found imitators in the viceroys and nobles, and the most flagitious and wicked acts were resorted to, with the object of handing over the lands of Ireland to the chief "adventurers." A nation of landholders or owners was converted into a nation of serfs or outlaws, and when fomenting rebellion and hatching plots did not suffice, religious animosity was enkindled, and the most odious acts were perpetrated in the sacred name of religion. Well may we exclaim, "Oh, religion, what infamous acts are done in thy name!"

The outrages perpetrated by the new upon the old landholders led to a class of offences which are called "agrarian." They proceed from a combination of those who think they have been wronged, and who seek by mutual protection to revenge the injuries perpetrated on them in the name of law. Many of the new "proprietors" proceeded to "clear" their lands, *i. e.*, to expel the occupants, in order to throw several small farms into a large one. This was resented, and as early as 1760 an outbreak of this character, under the name of the "Levellers," took place in Munster. Gordon, in his History of Ireland, says,—

"It was occasioned by *the expulsion of great numbers of labouring peasants*, destitute of any regular means of subsistence by any other species of industry: numbers of them secretly assembled in the night, and vented their fury on objects ignorantly conceived to be the causes of their misery."

Then followed the "Hearts of Oak," "Hearts of Steel," and "Peep-o'-Day Boys."

"This insurrection was excited by the conduct of *the middlemen, who demanded excessive fines, and racked the old tenants* to an extent utterly beyond their power to pay; they were of course 'cleared.'"

I do not wish you to accept my *ipse dixit* as to this condition of the Irish landholders and farmers during this period, and will therefore give you the *ipsissima verba* of some contemporary writers.

Lord Taaffe, writing in 1766, thus describes the effect of the laws upon the condition of the people :—

"The Catholics keep their farms in a bad plight, as they are excluded by law from durable and profitable tenures."

Lord Macartney in 1773 says,—

"If a Papist becomes a farmer, he shall not cultivate or improve his possession, being discouraged by the short limitation of his tenure; and yet we complain of the dulness and laziness of a people whose spirit is restrained from exertion, and whose industry has no reward to excite it."

Arthur Young, in his Tour in Ireland in 1777, gives the following list of the penal statutes respecting land in Ireland, which were then in force :—

"Catholics were incapacitated from purchasing land.
,, from lending money on mortgage.
,, their estates went in gavel among their children.
,, "If one child abjures, he inherits the whole.
,, "If a son abjures, the father has no power
,, over his estate, but becomes a pensioner in favour of such son.

"No Catholic could take a house for more than thirty-one years, and the rent must be two-thirds of the full value, and he could not have a horse worth more than £5."

He adds, "The preceding catalogue is very imperfect. These laws have crushed all industry, and wrested most of the property from the Catholics."

The same traveller thus describes the condition of the Irish people in 1778:—

"A landlord in Ireland can scarcely invent an order which a servant labourer or cottier dares to refuse to execute. Nothing satisfies him but unlimited submission. Disrespect, or anything tending towards sauciness, he may punish with his cane or horsewhip with the most perfect security. A poor man would have his bones broken if he offered to lift his hand in his own defence. Knocking down is spoken of in the country in a manner that makes an Englishman stare. Landlords of consequence have assured us that many of the cottiers would think themselves honoured by having their wives and daughters sent for to the bed of their master—a mark of slavery which proves the oppression under which such people must live. Nay, I have heard anecdotes of the lives of people being made free with without any apprehension of the justice of a jury. But let it not be imagined that this is curious; formerly it happened every day, but the law gains ground. It must strike the most careless traveller to see whole strings of cars whipped into a ditch by a gentleman's footman to make way for his carriage; if they are overturned or broken to pieces, no matter, it is taken in patience; were they to complain, they would perhaps be horsewhipped. The execution of the laws lies very much in the hands of the justices of the peace, many of whom are drawn from the most illiberal class of the kingdom. If a poor man lodges his complaint against a gentleman, or any animal that chooses to call himself a gentleman, and the justice issues out a summons for appearance, it is a fixed affront, and he will infallibly be *called out*. Where *manners* are in conspiracy against law, to whom are the opposed people to have recourse? It is a fact that a poor man having a contest with a gentleman—— but I am talking nonsense; they know their situation too well to think of that; they can have no defence but by means of protection from one gentleman against another, who probably protects his vassal as he would the sheep he intends to eat."

William Pitt spoke thus of the legislative policy of England towards Ireland previously to 1782:—

"The system has been that of debarring Ireland from the enjoyment and use of her resources, to make that kingdom completely subservient to the interest and opulence of this country (England) without suffering her to share in the *bounties of nature* and the industry of her citizens, or making them contribute to the general interests and strength of the empire. This system of cruel and abominable restraint has been exploded."

Mr. Fitzgibbon (afterwards Lord Clare), when attorney-general, declared in the Irish House of Commons in 1786,—

"Although tithes had been mentioned as the cause of the insurrection, yet such was not the fact, but that it arose from *the peasants being ground down to powder by exorbitant rents*, and who were so far from being able to pay their dues to the clergy that they possessed not food nor raiment for themselves."

Wakefield and Young, 1780, say with regard to Ireland that it would require an expenditure of £120,000,000 to bring its cultivation up to a level with that of the neighbouring island of Great Britain,* and that the average rent of the surface is only 17s. an English acre.†

The *Dublin Evening Post* for July 15th, 1786, says,—

"No kingdom perhaps experiences the want of a yeomanry in the degree that Ireland does. To the traveller no ranks are distinguishable save that of the *rabble* and the *gentry*."

Mr. Tighe, of Woodstock, in 1802, adds,—

"The bad state and deficiency of agricultural buildings, and the unimproved condition of many farms, may arise from various causes. First, nothing is ever built or repaired by the landlords. These expenses, as well as every other improvement, are left to the tenant, who generally comes into a dilapidated holding without capital enough to stock it, still less to build, to fence, to drain. Second, there is often a want of confidence between proprietor and occupier."

Alison observes (vol. i., p. 502),—

"Without doubt the first circumstance which contributed to produce the low standard of comfort and unbounded disposition to increase in the Irish poor was their subjugation to a foreign nation who did not *make their island the chief state of government*. The example of the Norman conquest of England is a decisive proof that such a conquest, if effected of so considerable a country as to occupy the first care and become wound up with the highest interests

* Young's "Ireland," ii., 9. † Wakefield, i., 585.

of the victor, is not only nowise inconsistent with subsequent prosperity, but may become a principal element in its formation. But the case is widely different when the conquest is effected of a country which governs its acquisition as a province. What Hungary is to Austria, and Poland to Russia, that Ireland has long been to Great Britain."

Wakefield, in his "Account of Ireland," says,—

"The hapless peasants gave way to the impulse of their ungovernable passions, and vented their fury on those whom they considered as their oppressors. These commotions afford a striking and melancholy proof of the state of the country at the time they took place, and as they arose from causes unconnected with public measures may convince those who ascribe every evil they experience to the government that national misfortunes depend more on the conduct of individuals than is generally believed or admitted."

Amongst the measures for the relaxation of the penal laws passed by the Irish parliament was one which affected the size of the holdings. The power of voting was given to Roman Catholic forty-shilling freeholders. The Irish party in the Irish parliament argued that it would be wiser to give greater political power to the Roman Catholic gentry, and they urged that the boon given to the uneducated classes would be used to obtain the rights which were withheld. This prophecy was fulfilled, but the agitation for complete Emancipation diverted the energies of the people from the advancement of their material interests. The creation of the forty-shilling freeholders led to a great breaking up of lands, and the fostering of a class of small holders, who, when that franchise was virtually destroyed, were swept off the lands.

The Act of Union greatly increased absenteeism, and encouraged that bane of a country, middlemen; the Irish peers who had town residences in Dublin, and who spent the portion of the year unoccupied by parliamentary duties on their estates, gave up the former, and became denizens of London: many of them rarely visited their Irish estates. This absence from Ireland destroyed many of the smaller industries in Ireland. The woollen manufactures, which were flourishing in 1800, had nearly disappeared in 1820, and the price of Irish wool greatly declined.* The increase in the taxation of Ireland after the Union had a material influence upon the condition of the farming classes.

The causes which originally produced the bad understanding between landlord and tenant are described as follows in the Report of the Devon Commission :—

"In 1793 was passed a further enactment, which materially affected the position of landlord and tenant. The forty-shilling franchise was by that Act extended to Roman Catholics; the landlords, as middlemen, then found the importance of a numerous following of tenantry, and subdivision and subletting, being by this law indirectly encouraged, greatly increased. The war with France raised considerably the profits of the occupier, who was thus enabled to pay a large rent to the mesne lessee. These causes produced throughout the country a class of intermediate proprietors, known by the name of middlemen, whose decline after the cessation of the war and the fall of prices in 1815, brought with it much of the evils we have witnessed of late years. Many who during the long war had amassed much wealth had become proprietors in fee; others who had not been so successful struggled in after years to maintain a position in society which their failing resources could not support.

* The change which had taken place in the agriculture of Ireland is shown in the following :—

Corn imported on an average of six years ending 1725.
Population, 2,300,000, or 71 on a square mile.

	Qrs.
Wheat	37,048
Barley and malt	7,255
Malted do.	677
Flour	4,083
Total	39,063

Total value of imports at prices of 1821, £78,126.

Corn exported in 1821.
Population, 6,801,827, or 211 on a square mile.

	Qrs.
Wheat	1,038,937
Oats	959,474
Barley	78,588
Meal (wheat)	252,010
Oatmeal	37,156
Total value of exports	£2,366,165

The number of cattle at Ballinasloe fair in 1799 was 9,157; in 1820 they were 8,505. The number of sheep in 1799 was 77,937; in 1820 it was 80,776.

Their sub-tenants were unable to pay 'war rents.' The middleman himself, who had come under rent during the same period, became equally unable to meet his engagements. All became impoverished; the middleman parted with his interest, or underlet the little land he had hitherto retained in his own hands: himself and his family were involved rapidly in ruin. The landlord, in many cases, was obliged to look to the occupier for his rent, or, at the expiration of the lease, found the farms covered with a pauper, and, it may be, a superabundant population. Subsequently the Act of 1829 destroyed the political value of the forty-shilling freeholder, and to relieve his property from the burden which this chain of circumstances brought upon it, the landlord in too many instances adopted what has been called the 'clearance system.'"

The Rebellion of 1798 would never have attained its prominence, were it not that the agrarian laws were so oppressive to the occupiers. It was the wrongs of the peasantry which afforded the bases upon which the agitators raised their superstructure of revolution. Subsequently to the Union the effort to repair injustice by violence and to remedy the inequality of law by lawlessness continued. In 1806 there were serious disturbances of a Whiteboy character in Connaught, which required special commissions to try them. It was stated by Chief Justice Downes and the law officers of the Crown, that the movement "was equally directed against the parson's tithe and the priest's dues; regulating the price of land and the wages of labour, not partaking of any political complexion, or confined to any particular party or persuasion of the people."

In 1811 disturbances again broke out in Leinster and Munster. Lord Chief Justice Norbury and Lord Guillamore describe them as "originating in disputes about land, opposition to tithes, and regulating wages; the avowed object being the regulation of landed property and its produce, to fix a maximum rent, prescribe the price of labour, and prevent the transfer of property."

Sir Robert Peel, in 1817, thus described the state of Ireland:—

"The evil which it is now proposed to remedy has not, I am sorry to say, risen on a sudden; it had existed for a considerable time,—

indeed, I might say for the whole period I had the honour of forming a part of the Irish Government. The disturbances in this county (Westmeath) appear to have commenced about the beginning of the year 1813, and have been rapidly increasing ever since, notwithstanding great exertions have been used on the part of the magistracy to check and subdue them; their objects appear to be that of regulating the price of ground set in con acre, and to prevent old tenants from being turned out of their farms."

Mr. James Daly, M.P. for Galway in 1820, thus described the condition of that county :—

"The state of disaffection and disturbance to which Ireland has been constantly subject for the last sixty years might be in a great degree attributed to the melancholy condition of the lower orders of its population. In a country which was for the most part destitute of manufactures, the population was almost entirely employed in the cultivation of the soil, and much of the existing disturbances had arisen from the large sums offered to landowners by the tenantry by which proprietors had unfortunately suffered themselves to be tempted, but which it was wholly beyond the means of the tenant to pay."

The laws of a country must be very defective when the people become dissatisfied and discontented and when they are living in open defiance to the law. I doubt if Prussia was about this period in as bad a state as Ireland, yet Count Hardenberg, in order to satisfy the people and to strengthen and consolidate the kingdom, gave those who were tenants-at-will one-half of their farms in fee, and to those who had a lease for years or for life he gave two-thirds of their holdings. This arbitrary Act, instead of diminishing the wealth of the proprietors, increased it; in less than five years the remaining portion became more valuable than the whole had been. The Irish farmers did not seek any such confiscation, they looked for permanence in their farms at a fixed rent. Had this been granted they would have improved their farms, but the landlords claimed a reversion in the labour of the occupier. They wished to preserve the power of evicting the tenant and taking possession of his improvements, or, what was equally unjust, of making him pay an increased rent on account of his own improvements. The consequence of this greed was, they prevented an outlay upon the land, and retarded the advancement of the country.

Grattan, in a speech delivered in 1814, thus refers to the change which took place in Irish agriculture and commerce. He said:—

"You know that it was the policy of your ancestors to destroy the manufactures of Ireland, and it was the tendency of the Union to direct her capital to gross produce. You have thus driven Ireland out of manufacture, and do you now propose to drive her out of tillage? You recollect that Ireland has for ages excluded the manufactures of other countries, and given an exclusive preference to yours. Ireland desires, and desires of right, that as she prefers your manufactures you should prefer her corn. Do you propose that Ireland should prefer the British manufacture, and that the British manufacturer should prefer the foreign husbandman?"

"Statistical Illustrations," page 60, inform us that—

"Ireland exported articles of subsistence alone to no less an amount (at the very reduced value of 1824) than £4,518,832; and in the three years, 1821, 1822, and 1823, to the enormous amount of upwards of £16,000,000, whilst nearly the whole of the remaining exports, to the amount of upwards of £10,000,000 more, in those three years were composed of the products of the Irish soil."

The absenteeism which the Act of Union extended, and the enormous taxation which it enforced, prevented the accumulation of capital. Poverty increased with taxation. The blank caused by the destruction of the Irish manufactures was not compensated by the increased growth of farm produce. The poor increased in number and in wretchedness. In 1819 their state became so pressing that a committee was appointed; its function was to inquire into and report upon the condition of the Irish labouring poor. This committee took much evidence. Its report briefly states that the poverty and wretchedness of the Irish poor was too apparent to require them to state the evidence which revealed it. The report ascribes the state of Ireland mainly to want of capital and want of employment; and it contains the following aphorism,—"Capital is the accumulation of savings which are the fruit of industry, which again is nourished and supported by its own progeny." These "fruits of industry" could not accumulate where the earnings of the working class were insufficient for their support, and where the drain from taxation carried off the profits of those classes who realized more than sufficed for their immediate wants. The committee recommended the extension of the linen trade to the south of Ireland, the promotion of the fisheries, the creation of piers and harbours as a means of affording employment and averting misery from the poor.

In 1823 another committee was appointed to inquire into the condition of the labouring poor, with a view to facilitate their employment in useful productive labour. Its report gives a sad and melancholy account of the condition of the poor; it repeats that it arises from want of capital, that this was the principal cause of the non-employment of the people, that the implements of agriculture were of the rudest sort, and there was not sufficient money in the hands of the farmers to pay the wages of the labourers, and it was set off against the rent of their cabins and small patches of land. In 1824 this committee was continued, and reiterated the same complaint.

In 1825 the House of Lords took up the subject, and appointed a committee, whose report says, "We have received a great body of evidence as to the actual state of the relations between landlord and tenant, and are of opinion that the whole of that most important subject is deserving the attentive consideration of Parliament."

The Irish nation had for nearly thirty years been much disturbed by the agitation for the removal of the penal laws. The inquiries which had taken place before the commissions of 1819, 1823, 1824, and 1825, had convinced Parliament that something was necessary to be done for Ireland. Sir Robert Peel, in 1829, proposed the measure of Catholic Emancipation. In introducing it to the House of Commons he gave the following melancholy picture of the mode of governing Ireland which had prevailed for thirty years. This statesman was eminently qualified to describe the legislative enactments, and to define their effects. He said—

"I apprehend that it is scarcely possible that we can change for the worse. What is the melancholy fact? That for scarcely one year during the period that has elapsed since the Union has Ireland been governed by the ordinary course of law. In 1800 we find the Habeas Corpus Act suspended, and the Act for the Suppression of Rebellion in force. In 1801 they were continued; in 1802, I believe they expired; in 1803 the insurrection for which Emmett suffered broke out; Lord Kilwarden was murdered by a savage mob, and both Acts of Parliament were renewed! In 1804 they were continued; in 1806 the west and south of Ireland were in a state of insubordination, which was with difficulty suppressed by the severest enforcement of the ordinary law. In 1807, in consequence chiefly of disorders that prevailed in 1806, the Act called the Insurrection Act was introduced; it gave power to the Lord Lieutenant to place any district by proclamation out of the pale of ordinary law; it suspended trial by jury, and made it a transportable offence to be out of doors from sunset to sunrise. In 1807 this Act continued in force, and in 1808-9, and to the close of the session of 1810. In 1814 the Insurrection Act was renewed; it was continued in 1815, 1816, and 1817. In 1822 it was again revived, and continued during the years 1823, 1824, and 1825. In 1825 the Act for the Suppression of Dangerous Associations was passed; it continued during 1826 and 1827, and expired in 1828."

The measure proposed by Sir Robert Peel became law The civil disabilities of the Roman Catholics were removed but the distress of the Irish people continued, though at the same time there were very large exports of food and other produce from the country.

A committee was again appointed in 1830; its inquiries occupied four months. The evidence of the wretchedness of the Irish people was voluminous and heartrending. The following extracts from the report express the views of this committee; they say,—

"A very considerable proportion of the population is considered to be out of employment; it is supposed to be from one-fifth to one-fourth. This, combined with the consequences of an altered system of managing land, is stated to produce *misery and suffering which no language can possibly describe*, and which it is necessary to witness in order fully to estimate. Their condition is necessarily most deplorable. It would be impossible for language to convey an idea of the state of distress to which the ejected tenantry have been reduced, or of the disease, misery, and even vice which they have propagated in the towns wherein they have settled, so that not only they who have been ejected have been miserable, but they have carried with them and propagated that misery. They have increased the stock of labour, they have rendered the habitations of those who received them more crowded, they have given occasion to the dissemination of disease, they have been obliged to resort to theft and all manner of vice and iniquity to procure subsistence; but what is, perhaps, the most painful of all, a vast number of them have perished of want. Your committee conceive that it is the imperative duty of individuals, of the Government, and of the Legislature, to consider what means can be devised to diminish this mass of suffering, and at the same time to secure the country a better economic condition, promoting a better management of estates, and *regulating the relations between landlord and tenant on rational and useful principles.*"

The report recommends the promotion of useful public works as a means of employment.

Mr. Roe, late secretary to the Dublin Chamber of Commerce, one of the most intelligent witnesses examined before that committee, sums up his evidence in the following words:—

"The operation of natural causes and an improved spirit of social life are the true and efficient sources from which the prosperity of Ireland may be anticipated;" and adds, "The foundations of her prosperity are laid, and time will complete the structure."

The same committee further reported that agriculture was improving, and commerce and internal trade were extending; though in the midst of abundant causes of good, there was still much want of employment and great misery in a portion both of the manufacturing and agricultural classes. They say—

"It would, however, be an error to conclude that the condition of the poorer classes had been improving in the same proportion, on the contrary, the committee find it stated on the high authority of the late Mr. Drummond, 'that whilst the country is making visible and steady progress in improvement, and signs of increasing wealth present themselves on all sides, the labouring population, constituting a large majority of the community, derive no proportionate benefit from the growing prosperity around them. In many places their condition is even worse than it had been.' The committee on the state of the poor in 1830 had noticed, as evidence of improvement in Ireland, extended cultivation, improved habits of industry, a better administration of justice, the re-establishment of peace and tranquillity in disturbed districts, and domestic colonization of the population in excess in certain places, a diminution of illicit distillation, and a very considerable increase to the revenue."

In 1832 another Committee of the House of Commons was appointed to consider the condition of the Irish labouring classes. Mr. Spring Rice, Lord Monteagle, subsequently Chancellor of the Exchequer, presided over its inquiries, which largely related to the fiscal and economic condition of Ireland. Their report says:

"The state of the labouring classes must mainly depend on the proportion existing between the people and the capital which can be profitably employed in labour. The removal of tenants from farms at the expiration of old leases is unquestionably a considerable cause of these disturbances, and the committee have considered the subject with a view, if possible, of getting rid of this source of evil." They recommended, "That whenever a landlord shall find it necessary to diminish the number of occupants on his estate, and be willing to give to the tenant, who has not the means of providing for himself when removed, a sum of money—as we trust a landlord will be always found willing to do—that then a further sum, bearing a fixed proportion to that given by the landlord, shall be applied to the use of the tenant, out of some other fund, to assist him to emigrate, or in whatever other way it may seem, on further consideration of the legislature, to be more advisable to apply to the grant of sums for the advantage of the tenant and the interest of the public."

They recognise the vast effect upon the whole fabric of society which is involved in the agrarian laws of the country, and recommend—

"An inquiry into the relations which exist between *landlord and tenant*, the connexion between the inheritor and the occupier of the soil being one which must influence, if not control, the whole system of society."

In 1833 the system of national education was introduced. It was anticipated that an extension of education would take place, and that an improvement in the tillage of the soil and in the condition of the people would follow. That system has been in operation for more than forty years; it has cost the country several millions, but the number of persons in Ireland who were able to read was less when the census was taken in 1861 than it had been in 1841, thus proving that the effect of the national system, has so far, been more negative than positive. The number unable to read has been lessened by several causes since 1841, but the number of those so far educated as to be able to read has not increased, nor has the tillage improved—the land has been going out of tilth.

In the "Life of Lord George Bentinck," by Lord Beaconsfield, at page 125, in alluding to assassinations and other violent crimes committed in Ireland, he states that—

"These barbarous distempers had their origin in the tenure of land in Ireland and in the modes of its occupation ; that soil has become divided into minute allotments, held by pauper tenants and at exorbitant rents, and by a class of middlemen, who were themselves necessitous and mere traders in land."

"Major" Vokes (whose interesting biography was written by his son-in-law, Lieut.-Colonel Addison) expressed himself to the following effect :—

"What I now say to you, sir, would cost me my coat or pension, but, nevertheless, from the experience of half a century, I am decidedly of opinion that had it not been for the shooting of agents and landlords now and then, it would, as the land laws stand, be impossible for the poor to live in this country."

During the reigns of the Georges I. and II., and part of that of George III., the Irish people had little, if any, influence in the direction of their own affairs. A faint gleam of prosperity arose during the seventeen years (1783 to 1800) in which the Irish Parliament was independent, but English influence was used to prevent the projected reform of the Irish representation, which would have given the Irish people a real voice in their own affairs. The Act of Union reduced Ireland to a province, and placed the responsibility of its good government upon British shoulders. In assuming the sole right to legislate for Ireland, the British people were morally bound to see that it was governed equitably, and that its people were made prosperous and happy. The history of the economic condition of Ireland, and of the state of the farmers and labourers, which I have drawn, not from sources coloured with Hibernian feeling, but from the records of the Imperial Parliament, proves that the British people, whose representatives were five-sixths of the British Legislature, either did not comprehend, or were unable to cope with, the evils of Irish misrule, arising mainly from the confiscation of the lands of the ancient Irish owners, the conferring of them upon those wholly unfit for such a trust, the inability or disinclination of a Parliament of landlords to curb the passions of their own class, and as a finale to this sad record of mis-legislation, the driving of the poor to seek that remedy which the laws under which they lived did not afford. It is sad to think that a peace-loving people were driven to resort to the wild justice of revenge, and that the legislation of seven hundred years produced no better effect than that so pithily described by such a competent witness as Major Vokes: "I am decidedly of opinion that, had it not been for the shooting of agents and landlords now and then, it would, as the land laws stand, be impossible for the poor to live in the country." Can I add a word to this pregnant epitome of misrule given by a police magistrate of great experience, and which is so condemnatory of the legislation of the Hanoverian sovereigns?

VI.—The Present.

The boasted civilization of the nineteenth century and the mild rule of the last of the Hanoverian sovereigns have not done much to ameliorate the condition of Ireland, or to place the ownership of the soil upon a sounder basis. Social changes have been effected. The poor, who heretofore wandered about and were supported by alms, have been immured in workhouses, and been supported by compulsory taxation. Vast numbers perished from famine, and still greater multitudes have been forced to seek in another country the employment or sustenance which was denied them in their own land.

One of the measures passed in the present reign which affected land and landholding in Ireland was the introduction of the Poor Law. This mode of providing for the poor had gradually grown up in England during the Tudor reigns. The first attempt was made in the reign of Henry VII., but the matured system was based upon an Act passed towards the close of that of Queen Elizabeth.*

In 1834 a commission of inquiry was appointed in relation to the Irish poor, with the preconceived intention of introducing the poor laws into Ireland. Its inquiries lasted until 1836. With reference to the labouring population the report says—

"A great portion of them are insufficiently provided with the commonest necessaries of life. Their habitations are wretched hovels; several of a family sleep together upon straw, or upon the bare ground, sometimes with a blanket, sometimes even without so much to cover them. Their food commonly consists of dry potatoes, and with these they are at times so scantily supplied as to be obliged to stint themselves to one spare meal in the day. There are even instances of persons being driven by hunger to seek sustenance in wild herbs. They sometimes get a herring or a little milk, but they never get meat except at Christmas, Easter, and Shrovetide. Some go to Great Britain in search of employment; others wander through Ireland with the same view. The wives and children of many have occasionally to beg. They do so reluctantly and with shame, and in general go to a distance from home, that they may not be known."

This commission recommended the formation of a board with comprehensive powers for national improvement. It was to undertake the improvement of waste lands, draining and fencing when necessary, the granting power to all tenants-for-life, to give leases for thirty-one years, the removal of cabins which are nuisances, the landlord contributing to the cost of removing the occupants to the improved land, and providing for them, and the construction of roads, bridges, and other means of internal communication. This report was thrown aside, and under the advice of Mr. Nicholls, an English gentleman, the system of poor laws was introduced. The building of the workhouses was not generally completed until 1842, when it may be said this measure was put upon trial.

The cost in 1842 was £281,233, in 1845 it was £316,123. The potato famine greatly increased the claims upon it, and the maximum was reached in 1859, when the charge was

* See History of Landholding in England, p. 67 *et seq.*

£1,674,793. In 1859 it had fallen to £413,712; it has since nearly doubled, and the amount raised in 1874 was £817,281. The Irish Poor Law differs in two essentials from that of England. First, there is no law of settlement, and next a moiety of the amount paid falls on the occupier, and the other moiety upon the rent. As to its effects, the Poor Law in Ireland in the reign of Victoria was but a rehearsal of that which took place in England in that of Elizabeth. It led to the "clearing of the land"—*i. e.*, the removal of the tenantry from their holdings. We have the testimony of Sir Matthew Barrington, in a letter written in 1844 to Sir Robert Peel, in which he remarks that "the landlords are rapidly clearing their estates, in apprehension of the effects of the Poor Law." A measure humane in its intention became the means of creating the pauperism for which it was intended to provide.

The landlords who passed the measure, fearful that the tax would diminish their incomes, expelled the labourers from their estates, and pulled down their houses. The homeless population was forced into the towns, and thus, there being no law of settlement, a burthen was transferred from the land, which ought to have borne it, to the industrial trading classes in the towns, and it required more than thirty years' agitation even to repair in degree the injury thus done.

The population of Ireland may be thus divided:—

	1841.	1871.
Towns of over 2,000 inhabitants	1,137,518	1,257,356
Rest of Ireland	7,037,606	4,151,403
Total	8,175,124	5,408,759

The increase in the urban population is mainly due to the operation of the Poor Laws, the decrease in the rural portion to other causes in connection with them.

In 1839 the House of Lords appointed a committee, which examined many witnesses upon the state of Ireland, but it could not agree to a report, and merely published four massive volumes of evidence, which it recommended to the serious attention of the House.

The taking the census in 1841 was availed of to ascertain the number of occupiers of land in Ireland and the quantity of live stock. The farms were classified, and it was found that there were 523,153 holdings under 15 acres each, and 127,961 over fifteen acres. About one-half of the live stock was owned by the smaller class of holders. The particulars, as stated by the Census Commissioners, are given in a foot note.*

The number of cattle in Ireland in 1841 was not quite as much as that at which was estimated in 1172, when Henry II. landed in that country. Cattle and sheep were less than the estimate made by Sir William Petty in 1670. The exports of cattle in 1841 may be estimated at 150,000, of sheep at 400,000, of live pigs at 1,000,000, of pigs in bacon and pork at 400,000. The imports of Irish butter into the ports of London and Liverpool were 624,301 firkins. The average exports of grain from Ireland in the five years from 1840 to 1845 were 2,622,825 quarters, and the total value of the exports of farm produce is stated to have been £12,000,000; of this about

* The number of holdings and the value of stock in 1841 was as under:—

Class of Holdings.	No. of Holdings.	Value of Stock.	Average value of Stock per Holding.
Under 1 acre	not given	£1,705,965	
Above 1 to 5 acres	310,375	3,065,529	£9 17 6
„ 5 to 15 acres	212,778	5,706,990	22 11 7
Total under 15 acres	523,153	10,478,484	
Above 15 to 30 acres	79,338	3,683,864	46 8 7
„ 30 acres	48,623	6,943,460	142 16 1
Total	651,114	21,105,808	

The live stock was apportioned among the different classes of holdings thus:—

	Horses and Mules.	Cattle.	Sheep.	Pigs.	Poultry.
Under 1 acre	39,144	102,052	123,060	282,822	2,087,706
Above 1 to 5 acres	83,070	268,422	235,130	254,483	1,796,712
„ 5 to 15 „	177,728	511,489	402,354	352,845	2,310,407
„ 15 to 20 „	112,991	331,028	294,796	215,973	1,145,915
„ 20 acres	153,183	650,043	1,050,775	240,993	1,107,148
	561,116	1,863,034	2,106,115	1,347,116	8,447,888

£4,000,000 was retained in England as absentee rents. Ireland took British manufactures or foreign commodities for the remaining £8,000,000.

In 1842 Sir Robert Peel succeeded to office, and in the following year he appointed a commission, which, having been presided over by the Earl of Devon, was known as the Devon Commission. Its labours commenced in 1843, and the report was issued in 1845. It visited various parts of Ireland, and took evidence from witnesses in different grades of society. The report indicates the want of proper regulations between landlord and tenant. It says—

"The Irish peasant is still badly housed, badly fed, badly clothed, and badly paid for his labour. It would be impossible to describe adequately the privations which they and their families habitually and patiently endure. It will be seen in the evidence that in many districts their only food is the potato, their only beverage water; that their cabins are seldom a protection against the weather, that a bed or a blanket is a rare luxury, and that in nearly all their pig and manure heap constitute their only property. When we consider this state of things, and the large proportion of the population which comes under the designation of agricultural labourers, we have to repeat that the patient endurance they exhibit is deserving of high commendation, and entitles them to the best attention of Government and of Parliament. Their condition has engaged our most anxious consideration. Up to this period any improvement which has taken place is attributable almost entirely to the habits of temperance in which they have so generally persevered, and not, we grieve to say, to any increased demand for their labour. The obvious remedy for this state of things is to provide remunerative employment, which may at once increase the productive powers of the country and improve the condition of the people."

The object for which this commission was appointed was to inquire into the state of the law and practice in respect to the occupation of lands, and to report as to the best means of encouraging a better system of agriculture, and to improve the relations between landlord and tenant. They say in their report—

"We believe at no former period did so active a spirit of employment prevail, nor could well-directed measures for the attainment of that object have been proposed with a better prospect of success than at the present moment. We regret, however, to be obliged to add that in most parts of Ireland there seems to be no corresponding advance in the condition and comforts of the labouring classes. A reference to the evidence of most of the witnesses will show that the agricultural labourer of Ireland continues to suffer the greatest privations and hardships. Our personal experience and observations during our inquiry have afforded us a melancholy confirmation of these statements, and we cannot forbear expressing our strong sense of the patient endurance which the labouring classes have generally exhibited under sufferings greater we believe than the people of any country in Europe have to sustain."

Sir Matthew Barrington, addressed a letter to Sir Robert Peel in 1844, and thus described the state of this country :—

"In Ireland land is concentrated in the hands of a few large proprietors, while nearly all the intermediate cultivators and occupants are either tenants at will or possessed of short leases rapidly expiring. This principle of tenure, which gives the possessor no security, and but little interest in his holding, and deprives him of the hope of any prospective amelioration of his condition,—this it is that renders the Irish peasant reckless, inconsiderate and improvident; results that are in accordance with the universally admitted principle, that the institution of property is the basis of civilization, and that a variation in the amount of security or interest therein exercises a corresponding influence upon the moral and social condition of the people. Nearly two-thirds of the whole of the lands of Ireland has lately fallen out of lease, and are now held by occupiers at will. The landlords are rapidly *clearing* their estates in apprehension of the effect of the Poor Law, and there being but few manufactures in the country, the support and existence almost of the peasant depend on his quarter of an acre of potato ground; deprive him of this, or let his possession be uncertain, and what interest has he in preserving the peace of the country?"

The letter is remarkable from the fact that it was written two years before the appearance of the potato blight. The Select Committee on the Irish Poor had in the previous year reported as to the allotment system; they said "it gives the working man something which he may call his own; and as its value depends on his own exertions, it prompts him to the exercise of self-control, and leads him to look on from the present towards the future. It furnishes him with an interest in life, to stimulate his faculties, to occupy his mind, and to inspire him with hope ; and it becomes a powerful inducement to abstain from any of those offences which would lead to a forfeiture of the valued possession. It gives him a feeling of independence and self-respect ; it gives him a stake in the country, and places him in the class which has something to lose."

In 1846 two circumstances occurred which greatly influenced land in Ireland: one was the potato blight, the other the alteration in the corn laws. The former occasioned a fearful temporary evil, the latter caused permanent and very extraordinary results. The growth of grain for the English market had occupied a large portion of the soil of Ireland, and given employment to vast numbers of the Irish people ; the grain so grown was manufactured in Ireland, and large milling concerns were erected, which gave a great amount of employment, and supplied a considerable quantity of coarse food for the people and offal for fattening pigs. The extent of the trade is shown by the continuous large export of grain, which in the five years from 1840 to 1845 was nearly 3,000,000 quarters per annum. The low prices which prevailed from 1848 to 1852 injured this branch of agriculture and manufacture, and there was a very great want of employment, and extensive emigration.

The potato disease which visited Ireland in 1846, 1847, and 1848, found the people completely unprepared. The smaller farmers were loaded with a disproportionate rent, and had embarked some of their earnings in the cottage that sheltered them ; they relied upon the potato for food ; the live stock which they possessed, which paid the rent and manured the grounds, was sufficient under prosperous circumstances, but they were compelled to sell their live stock at ruinously low prices to procure food, and were left without the means of tilling their farms or paying their rent. The number of small farms—those under 15 acres—diminished to one-half. The landlords, who had been living in many casse beyond their means, were loaded with debt, and unable to assist their tenantry, eviction followed non-payment of rent, and the sale of estates was a consequence.

Upon the appearance of the potato disease in 1846, Sir Robert Peel, who recognised the duty of Government to supply food to the people, purchased maize in large quantities in America and Turkey; he supplied it for gratuitous distribution at a limited price, and thus prevented excessive pressure from high prices upon other purchasers, and tided over the calamity, without much suffering.

In 1847 the disease again appeared with greater virulence. Sir Robert Peel had been replaced by Lord John Russell, the wise measures for feeding those who suffered from the loss of the potato were not continued. The supply of food was left to the ordinary operations of trade, and they proved very ruinous to the Irish farmers. Government became purchasers of food for gratuitous distribution in the local markets, and thus enhanced the price on those who tried to sustain themselves; had the same food been purchased abroad, as had been done by Sir Robert Peel, it would have saved one-half the capital of the small farmers.

The Committee of the House of Lords of 1852 estimated the loss in 1847 at £16,000,000. They say in their report,—

"The committee see reason to think that, with occasional exceptions, the improvement of Ireland in its material interest was progressive prior to the failure of crops in 1845. The last and most fearful crisis was produced through the dispensation of Providence in 1845 and the succeeding years, and more especially in the years 1846 and 1847. The amount of loss sustained in the produce of one single year is estimated by a witness, a high authority upon such subjects (Mr. Griffith), at the sum of £16,000,000 sterling."

The Irish farmers were neither indolent nor unthrifty. Mr., afterwards Sir Richard Griffith, estimated the value of the crops in 1846 at £51,250,000, or, on the average, about £4 per acre for the arable lands; of this, £43,000,000 was crops produced by tillage, the products of man's labour ; the number of producers of food at this time was 1,859,141, and the average produce of each person's labour would have been about £28.

In 1847 Government employed the constabulary to collect the statistics of Ireland, and the information so collected proves that the grain crop of Ireland in 1847 was sufficient to have sustained a population of nearly eighteen millions. Dr. Lyon Playfair has made the following calculation of the quantity of flesh-formers in the crop of Ireland of 1847 :—

"The statistics of Ireland of 1847 give the following in pounds of flesh-formers :—

	lbs.
Barley	575,148,575
Bere and Rye	2,610,274
Beans and Peas	6,224,256
Wheat	138,724,776
Oats	561,101,348
Potatoes	64,231,395
Total	1,348,040,624

He adds, "On an average, man, woman, and child consumes annually 62·2 lbs. of flesh-formers." If one-sixth be deducted for seed, it would leave 1,120,000,000 lbs. flesh-formers, or sufficient for eighteen millions people. If one-half the barley was used in brewing and distilling, and one-half the oats given to horses, and one-half the potatoes for fattening pigs, it would leave 626,000,000 lbs. flesh-formers, or sufficient for the sustenance of ten million people. The only measure that would have been necessary would have been to have prevented the export of grain from Ireland ; this would have left sufficient food for the wants of the people. It was not done, lest it should have interfered with the profits of speculators ; their advantage appeared of greater moment than the welfare of a nation.

The decrease in the population of Ireland, which took place

between 1841 and 1851,* was traced principally to the potato failure, but it continued at an equal ratio during the period from 1851 to 1861; and arose from a different cause. The alteration in the laws relating to foreign corn affected the cultivation of cereal crops; land in Ireland, which had previously been tilled, was put under pasture, and there was a great diminution in the area under culture. An idea became prevalent that it would be beneficial to the mass of the agriculturists of Ireland to deprive them of their holdings, and to convert them into paid labourers, and hence arose the notion that moral and physical regeneration would arise from consolidating farms and making the small farmers hired labourers. This idea, like other nostrums, had its day, but it was a day of mischief. Those who promoted it overlooked the fact, which is proved by the invariable experience of mankind of every age, and in every nation, that an increase in the size of farms is *per se* a diminution in the quantity of produce, and that men cannot be elevated by reducing them from the independence of farmers, however small the size of their holdings, to the

* The following are the various estimates and returns of the population of Ireland:—

Year	Source	Population
1672	Sir William Petty*.	1,100,000
1695	Capt. South	1,034,102
1712	Hearth-money collection	2,0990,94
1718	,, ,,	2,169,048
1725	,, ,,	2,317,374
1731	Established clergy	2,010,221
1754	Hearth-money collection	2,372,634
1767	,, ,,	2,544,276
1777	,, ,,	2,690,556
1785	,, ,,	2,845,932
1788	Gervas P. Bushe, Esq.	4,040,000
1791	Hearth-money collection	4,206,612
1792	Dr. Beaufort	4,088,026
1805	Thos. Leiruhen	5,395,426
1814	Parliamentary return	5,937,856
1821	,, ,,	6,801,827
1831	,, ,,	7,767,401
1841	,, ,,	8,196,597
1851	,, ,,	6,574,278
1861	,, ,,	5,798,967
1871	,, ,,	5,402,759

* Sir William Petty states that the population of Ireland had, during the wars of the previous twenty years, been reduced by 500,000.

dependence of labourers, however well paid. The history of the agriculture of Ireland is another illustration of this fact; as the number of holdings lessens, so does the area under cultivation diminish, and as the quantity of land under tillage narrowed, and employment became circumscribed, emigration increased and population diminished.

Parliamentary returns show that, while over 80 per cent. of small holdings is tilled, less than 40 per cent. of that of large holdings is cultivated. The number of holdings in Ireland reduced from 691,202 in 1841* to 534,024 in 1871, the decrease in that period being 157,178, but in the small farms, which yielded the largest produce, the diminution was from 563,235 in 1841 to 236,057 in 1861, the decrease being 327,178. Each of these holdings represented a family of five persons, or a population of 535,896.

The area under tillage has diminished very considerably, the extent under cereals was reduced from 3,313,595 acres in 1847 to 1,848,487 in 1876, the land under potatoes also was less, and though the increase in cattle led to a greater cultivation of green crops, yet the total area under cultivation had fallen from 4,767,191 acres in 1847 to 3,211,701 acres in 1876, the decrease being 1,556,490 acres, or 30 per cent.†

The deplorable result which was produced by the legislation

* The number of holdings in 1841 and 1871 was as follows:—

	1841.	1875.
Above 1 and under 5 acres	310,436	69,098
„ 5 „ 15 „	252,799	166,959
	563,235	236,057
„ 15 „ 30 „	79,342	137,699
„ 30 „	48,625	—
	691,202	534,024
Decrease	... ...	157,178

† Quantity of land under crops:—

	Under cereal crops. Acres.	Under potatoes.	Under green crops.	Total.	Population.
1847	3,313,579	1,000,000	443,622	4,767,191	8,175,124
1851	3,099,401	868,501	483,814	4,451,716	6,551,970
1861	2,623,683	1,133,801	437,467	4,394,351	5,764,543
1871	2,124,079	1,058,287	453,244	3,635,600	5,402,759
1876	1,848,487	880,693	482,531	3,211,701	

of 1846 was felt most heavily in those districts which had been devoted to the culture of grain for sale. The rent of these farms was principally paid out of cereal crops. These crops were produced by the labour of the tenant, and it was upon his labour that the rent-receiving classes depended. The free importation of grain had the effect of running the agriculturists of this country, who were loaded with the support of the rent-receiving classes, against the agriculturists of other countries, where, the tenant being the proprietor, he had no such burthen. A farmer in Ireland found that he could not produce grain as cheaply as a farmer in America or Russia, where the cost is only the seed and labour; he found also that he could not live in the race of competition, because he had to give a portion of the produce to a man who merely received the rent, while the foreign farmer kept it all for himself. Irishmen discovered that they could not earn a livelihood in Ireland by growing grain for the British markets, though accessible in twelve hours, but that they could accumulate property by growing grain for the British market in America, 3,000 miles away; they therefore took their labour and capital to that country.

The change in the corn laws led to a more startling innovation. Lands which should be farmed in such a way as to produce the largest quantity of food for the people of the country, came to be cultivated with a different object,—that was to yield the greatest amount of rent to the landlord. Men were deprived of home-grown food in order that landlords might increase their rent-rolls. It is quite possible to lessen the outlay for labour upon a farm, to diminish the area under tillage, to decrease the quantity of its crops, and yet increase the rent.*

The quantity of cereal produce in 1875, a very favourable

"One only master grasps the whole domain,
And *half* a tillage *stints* the smiling plain."—*Goldsmith*.

* The following figures, extracted from Government returns, show the change :—

		Quantity of cereals. Qrs.	Quantity of potatoes. Tons.	Quantity of green crops. Tons.
1847	produce	16,248,934	2,048,195	6,736,949
1851	,,	14,184,066	1,142,043	7,140,381
1861	,,	9,618,098	1,858,433	4,939,429
1871	,,	9,082,464	2,793,641	5,008,295
1875	,,	9,966,355	3,512,884	6,441,462

year, was 6,282,579 quarters less than that of 1847. The crop of 1875 comprised 552,417 quarters wheat, 8,203,707 quarters oats, 1,176,194 quarters barley, 4,026 quarters peas, and 30,011 quarters rye. Ireland used to be regarded as the granary of England ; now she does not grow enough for her own use.*

The population of Ireland in 1845 was 8,250,000, the exports of grain from that country in 1845 represents 3,000,000 quarters, or sufficient to feed three millions in excess of the population. The imports were *nil*. After a lapse of thirty years the population had fallen to 5,402,759. The number of persons to be fed had lessened by 2,772,365, yet the exports had not increased, in 1875 they were 1,618,865 quarters, while the imports amounted to 4,170,993 quarters, or 2,452,128 quarters in excess of the exports. The former surplus disappeared, and there was in its stead a large deficit.

The diminution of the population of the rural districts is nearly three millions ; whether this decrease is solely owing to the alteration in the corn laws is a debatable question. The production of grain lessened, land without labour must remain untilled. The effect of throwing the land out of tillage has been to increase the quantity of live stock :—

"Beasts accumulate as men decay."†

* The shipments of grain from Ireland in 1845 and 1875 were as under :—

	Wheat. Qrs.	Oats. Qrs.	Barley. Qrs.	Beans & Peas. Qrs.	Malt. Qrs.	Oatmeal. Cwts.	Flour. Cwts.
1845	371,000	1,678,000	92,000	14,300	11,000	1,058,000	1,421,000
1875	12,697	970,076	56,025	17,786	1,815	460,466	217,499
Decrease	359,303	707,924	35,975		9,185	597,534	1,203,501

The imports of foreign and colonial grain into Ireland in 1845 and 1875 were as under :—

	Wheat. Qrs.	Oats. Qrs.	Barley. Qrs.	Rye. Qrs.	Maize. Qrs.	Flour. Cwts.	Indian Meal. Cwts.
1845	*Nil.*						
1875	2,504,861	18,184	12,904	6,066	1,401,698	368,367	13,043

† The Government returns as to the number of live stock are as follows :—

	Horses and Mules.	Cattle.	Sheep.	Pigs.	Poultry.
1841	576,115	1,863,116	2,106,189	1,412,813	8,458,517
1851	543,312	2,967,461	2,122,128	1,084,857	7,470,694
1861	614,232	3,471,688	3,556,050	1,102,042	10,371,175
1871	537,633	3,973,102	4,228,721	1,616,754	11,717,182
1876	556,630	4,113,693	4,007,518	1,484,143	13,582,782

A legislative measure, the Parliamentary Voters' Act of 1850, has had a serious and deteriorating effect upon the system of landholding in Ireland. This enactment conferred the franchise upon all persons who have for twelve months been rated as occupiers of land or premises valued at £12 a year. This tended to diminish all tenancies in Ireland except those at will. The landlord of tenants-at-will reckoned on having greater political influence, he calculated on receiving the rent and commanding the vote of his tenant. If the occupier were either a freeholder or a leaseholder he would be more independent. He who desires to possess property, to enjoy the fruit of his labours, and to be really independent—and who is there that does not long for the enjoyment of these natural rights?—hastened to leave the country. He carries his labour and capital to those regions where he can become the owner of land, and has with that ownership all the privileges which follow upon such proprietary rights. The emigration from Ireland has continued to be very great, and it is stimulated by causes which might have been expected to prevent it. In the past twenty years the number of emigrants from Ireland has exceeded the entire population of some European states. Since 1846 it has been nearly three millions. Deficiency in the supply of labour has lessened the culture of the soil and the supply of food. The mode of farming has become more and more barbarous; the land which used to be tilled is converted into pasture; the production of cereals has diminished, the insufficient supply of winter food for cattle has lessened the production of meat and butter, and in their stead an exhaustive method, the rearing and shipment of young stock, has taken its place.* Depopulation has been produced by emigration, on this subject John Milton wrote:—

* There is a great increase in the export of cattle, but it principally consists of young animals which are fattened in England.

The live stock exported from Ireland was as follows:—

	Oxen, Bulls, and Cows.	Calves.	Sheep and Lambs	Pigs.
1846	186,483	6,363	259,257	480,827
1861	334,304	24,360	407,426	358,187
1871	423,396	60,520	684,708	528,244

"I shall believe there cannot be a more ill boding sign to a nation (God turn the omen from us) than when the inhabitants, to avoid insufferable grievances at home, are forced by heaps to forsake their native country."

Mr. Stuart Mill develops this idea at greater length. Writing in 1852, he says,—

"There can be little doubt that, however much the employment for agricultural labour may hereafter be diminished by the general introduction throughout Ireland of English farming, or even if, like the county of Sutherland, all Ireland should be turned into a grazing farm, the superseded people would migrate to America with the same rapidity, and as free of cost to the nation as the million of Irish who have gone thither during the last three years. Those who think that the land of a country exists for the sake of a few thousand landowners, and that as long as rents are paid, society and Government have fulfilled their function, may see in this consummation a happy end to Irish difficulties. But this is not a time, nor is the human mind now in a condition in which such insolent pretensions can be maintained. The land of Ireland, the land of every country, belongs to the people of the country. The individuals called landowners have no right in morality and justice to anything but rent, or compensation for its saleable value. With regard to the land itself, the paramount consideration is, by what mode of appropriation and of cultivation it can be made most useful to the collective body of its inhabitants. To the owners of rent it may be convenient that the bulk of the inhabitants, despairing of justice in the country where they and their ancestors lived and suffered, should seek on another continent that property in land which is denied to them at home. But the Legislature of the empire ought to regard with other eyes the forced expatriation of millions of people. When the inhabitants of a country quit the country *en masse* because its government will not make it a place fit to live in, the Government is judged and condemned. It is the duty of Parliament to reform the landed tenure of Ireland. There is no necessity of depriving the landlords of one farthing of the pecuniary value of their legal rights; but justice requires that the actual cultivators should be enabled to become in Ireland that which they will become in America,—proprietors of the soil which they cultivate."

Mr. Mill then proceeds to show that the condition of the

Irish people would not be ameliorated by converting them into receivers of wages, but that they would be raised by a proprietorship in land. "There is," he truly observes, "no stimulus as yet comparable to property in land."

The attention of Parliament has been turned to the question of ownership of land, both in Great Britain and Ireland, and returns have been prepared showing the number of owners, the area of their estates, and their value. The most recent with reference to Ireland is that presented to the House of Commons in August, 1876. It does not correspond with a return made on the same subject in 1870. The totals of each are—

	No. of Proprietors.	Area in Acres.	Valuation.
Return of 1870	19,228	20,047,572	£10,182,681
,, 1876	68,711	20,157,511	13,418,358

The later return includes owners of less than an acre, who number 36,144, who own an area of 9,065 acres, valued at £1,366,448; but even if these figures are deducted they do not reconcile the accounts. The return of 1876 appears to include house property, as the valuation corresponds with that of the entire of Ireland. The return of 1870 is given at foot.*

It is remarkable to note the decrease in the acreable valuation as the farms increase in size. The smallest size are about 33s. per acre, the next 22s., those from 50 to 100 acres 19s., and they gradually lessen until the largest estates are only 6s.

	No. of Proprietors.	Total Area.	Total Valuation.
* Under 25 acres	2,377	29,056	£47,187
Over 25 to 50	1,460	52,804	62,637
,, 50 to 100	2,082	152,004	144,441
	5,919	233,864	254,265
100 to 200	2,788	408,699	334,476
200 to 300	1,916	471,646	345,662
300 to 500	2,271	884,493	591,104
500 to 1,000	2,633	1,871,171	1,133,887
1,000 to 2,000	1,773	2,474,756	1,385,581
2,000 to 5,000	1,246	3,872,611	1,997,202
5,000 to 10,000	440	3,071,471	1,453,697
10,000 to 20,000	192	2,607,719	1,174,223
20,000 and upwards	110	4,151,142	1,512,594
	19,228	20,047,572	£10,182,681

per acre. The smallest ownerships are about 12 acres each, and if the whole of Ireland were as productive as these estates the valuation would be upwards of £30,000,000. I think it is possible by good farming to triple, or even quadruple, the amount of produce from the soil, but this desirable result can only be brought about by subdividing estates and increasing the number of proprietors.

The effect of the period of confiscation, to which I have already referred, was to transfer the bulk of the soil of Ireland from the descendants of the ancient Celtic race to the invaders. The extent to which this has been carried is shown in the peerage. There are now 187 Irish peers, but only five male descendants of Irish families have been raised to that position, that is, less than one thirty-fifth of the entire. It would follow that the landlordism of the country has undergone similar changes. "Ill got, ill gone," applies to many of these estates. The Norman, Tudor, Stuart, Cromwellian, and Williamite adventurers were reckless and profuse in their expenditure debts, mortgages, bonds, accumulated upon their estates, and when a Nemesis came in the famine of 1846-7, when rents were not paid and poor rates increased, they were unable to meet their demands. Evictions were carried out in so heartless a manner that a law was passed to prevent families being turned out of their houses on Christmas Day. The smaller class of holders, who relatively paid the highest rents, had been ejected. The Crowbar brigade was in full operation, and the country was studded with the bare walls of unroofed dwellings. The untilled land was in a short time covered with natural grasses and weeds, and the landlords, who lived upon the labour of the poor, were reduced to great straits. The oppression of mortgagees increased in severity, and it was evident " something should be done." History tells the same story of other countries: the land of the Jews in the time of Nehemiah was possessed by mortgagees ; the lands of the Athenians in the time of Solon, and those of Rome, under the Commonwealth, became subject to the "monetary interest." In each of these cases the land was freed from the load of debt, and the tillers of the soil, relieved of their burthen, were enabled to increase its produce.

English statesmen adopted for Ireland a course different from that sanctioned by precedent. Mammon, not justice, guided the legislature; the creditors, the mortgagees, were to be protected, the loss from the visitation of Providence might touch those who had bought land, but must not reach those who had lent money on it. The Incumbered Estates Court was the remedy applied to this evil of Ireland. It was based on the fallacy that it would bring capital into Ireland, whereas all the money paid for lands went to discharge debts. The amount received was precisely equal to the amount paid. It was previously an established legal principle that a puisne creditor—one who lent money upon land already mortgaged—could not sell the land without paying the prior mortgage in full; but that wise principle was overlooked, and in the desire "to do something," very great injustice was done to innocent parties. Land was forced into the market, and sold at ridiculously low rates, and a new class of landlords, who had "incumbered the estates" in embryo, mortgaged the land before they bought it, and paid off the existing mortgages by borrowing on the same security came into existence.

Bad as things were, there was on most estates a bond of kindly feeling between the old race of landlords and the tenants; they had grown up together, had hunted, fished, and coursed together, grey-headed landlords were to grey-headed tenants "Master Tom" or "Master Dick," the tenant looked upon his landlord as his friend. The new race were guidely solely by the £ s. d. principle; they had bought, and should get payment on their investments, hence the relation was without feeling, and the most heartless system was pursued in relation to the lands. Had the legislators of 1850 been wise, they would have introduced into the Incumbered Estates Act a provision as to the right of pre-emption by the tenant, similar to that which, at a later date, was introduced into the Irish Church Act, under which a tenant who pays one-fourth

of the value of his land is allowed to clear off the remainder
in thirty-two years. Those who had charges on land did not
want to be paid off, as they had to reinvest their money; they
wanted security and annual interest, and there was no insuper-
able difficulty in providing both. Land would have fetched a
higher price, the creditors would have been better off, and a
new class of landholders would have been created, who
would have altered the face of the country. All the good
effected by Stein and Hardenberg would have been produced without the confiscation ; but the opportunity was lost,
and, instead of creating a class of yeomen, farming their own
land, the state called into existence a class of petty land
speculators, who borrowed the money to purchase the land,
and were a sort of middlemen. The heartlessness with which
they managed their new purchases increased agrarian crime,
and rendered further legislation necessary.

The Irish Land Act of 1871 was but the supplement or the
complement of the Incumbered Estates Act of 1851. It was
based upon a right principle. It recognised the separate
estates in the land and the improvements made thereon, and
it also recognised an estate of occupation. Its defect lay in
these points,—it did not allow the owner of the improvements
to sell them in market overt, but compelled him to sell them
to the landlord at a price fixed on, not by a jury or by arbi-
trators, but by a single judge. It also limited the estate or
goodwill of the occupier to those who had not leases, holding
that the lease was a covenant to surrender on a stated day,
and that a man was not entitled to compensation for doing
that which he had contracted to perform. The Act failed,
however, to secure to the Irish tenant that which he sought,
undisturbed possession of his holding at a fair rent. Evictions
have increased since the Act was passed, and the feeling of
insecurity instead of diminishing has increased. The landlords find that they have to pay less than the value both for
disturbance and improvements, and instead of the Act imposing a penalty on them it gives them a bonus. They can
either in money or increased rent get a larger sum from the

incoming tenant than they paid the outgoing one, and in some cases the conduct of the landlords has been arbitrary, cruel, and unjust.

The desire for *Tenant Right* arises from the consciousness that the land belongs to the people, that it was not liable to rent, though subject to tribute. It springs from the tradition that at a time not very remote there was neither landlord nor rent. A man could not be evicted from his land. This cognate idea is expressed in the term " *Tenant Right.*" It is difficult to discover upon what principle of law, even as it was understood in the days of the Plantagenets, these monarchs took upon themselves to seize upon the lands of the Irish people and give them to their Norman followers. The right of the English monarch, was, at best, that gained by his subject Strongbow on his marriage with Eva Mac Murrough, and it did not *per se* give any right to seize upon the lands of the septs and give them to others. The submission of the Irish kings and chieftains did not *per se* give the English monarch any rights of forfeiture, or any of those powers arising out of investiture. A sovereign could only invest a man with that which was in his possession, and Henry II. did not possess the land of Ireland ; and he could only seize upon or forfeit that which *he* had given on the condition of allegiance and fealty. The kings of England did not fulfil the first condition of sovereignty, though repeatedly asked by the Irish to do so. They were asked to extend the laws of England to Ireland ; and as they did not establish the relation of suzerain and subject they did not acquire the right of forfeiture or sequestration, and their whole policy was not only wrong when judged by modern ideas of right and wrong, but it was unjust and inequitable when tried by the ethics of that time. The confusion and misery produced was very great, and for centuries the English monarch received no equivalent. A great wrong was perpetrated in the reign of James I. when the judges, without any case before them, without argument or right of appeal, passed a resolution which disturbed the title of a vast mass of the people to their lands.

The history of land tenure in Ireland, from the invasion of Henry II. to the present time, is an apt illustration of the evils which follow a course of pillage and spoliation. The ancient system of landholding under which Ireland had been prosperous, refined, civilized, and Christianized, received its first shock from the hordes of Danish pirates; its second from the Norman settlers of 1172. Wave after wave of emigrants, all greedy for the lands of Ireland, rolled over it in quick succession. The Plantagenets, the Tudors, the Stuarts, alike looked to spoliation in Ireland as the reward of their powerful subjects. Chichester, Wentworth, and Petty were unscrupulous instruments in carrying out a wicked policy. Cromwell and William of Orange, who are regarded in the sister country as champions of civil and religious liberty, appear in Ireland as sequestrators and spoliators. When feudalism disappeared, and men could no longer seize upon the property of others by open rapine, religious fanaticism was called in, and the pretence, that the possession of land by those who did not adopt the creed of the Reformation, was dangerous to liberty, was used as a cloak for despoiling many who still had estates in Ireland.

Ireland is a striking proof of the misery which follows from a career of rapine and spoliation. The laws relating to land tenure have prevented improvement, and kept the people in a barbarous and uncivilized state which is disgraceful to free institutions. A standing condemnation of these laws is found in the continuous exodus of its people. Ireland possesses great resources,—a genial climate, a fertile soil, capacious harbours, navigable rivers, a good position in the map of Europe; these advantages ought to make her rich and prosperous, and her people happy and contented: she is, however, poor and non-progressive, her people are restless and dissatisfied, and she will continue so until her laws are more equitable, and her land system is renovated by returning to the equitable system of the Brehon code.

BY THE SAME AUTHOR.

Octavo, price 3s. cloth,

HISTORY OF LANDHOLDING IN ENGLAND.

"This book, as might be expected from so eminent an authority, is drawn up with great care; abounds with much learning, and often puts well-known historical incidents in an original light."—*Land and Water.*

"Is a model of conciseness and accuracy."—*John Bull.*

"Really very interesting."—*Stamford Mercury.*

"An able and important book."—*Notes and Queries.*

"Of considerable value."—*Building News.*

"Pertinent and just."—*Athenæum.*

"Will be found especially interesting. Is temperately written and based on facts."—*English Mechanic.*

"A most useful work of reference on the important subject of landholding."—*Derbyshire Courier.*

"This work contains, in a small space, a large amount of information."—*Highlander.*

"Interesting and valuable. . . . Much readable matter is condensed into a small compass."—*Field.*

"Of great historical interest and usefulness."—*Hull News.*

"Most able and interesting."—*Irish Times.*

"Traces the system with a clearness which will be found valuable."—*Economist.*

Price 6s.,

THE FOOD SUPPLIES OF WESTERN EUROPE.

LONDON: LONGMANS, GREEN, AND CO.

Price 3s. 6d.,

THE CURSE OF IRELAND.

Being an Examination of the Treaty of Union between Great Britain and Ireland, and an Inquiry into the manner in which it has been carried out.

Price 1s.,

HOW IRELAND MAY BE SAVED.

LONDON: RIDGWAY.

MARCH 1877

CLASSIFIED LISTS OF BOOKS

(NEW WORKS AND NEW EDITIONS)

IN

MISCELLANEOUS

AND

GENERAL LITERATURE

FOLLOWED BY

AN ALPHABETICAL INDEX UNDER AUTHORS' NAMES

London
Longmans, Green & Co.
Paternoster Row
1877.

ANCIENT HISTORICAL EPOCHS.

Now in course of publication, uniform with EPOCHS of MODERN HISTORY, each volume complete in itself,

EPOCHS OF ANCIENT HISTORY:

A Series of Books Narrating the History of Greece and Rome and of their Relations to other Countries at Successive Epochs.

Edited by the Rev. GEORGE W. COX, M.A. late Scholar of Trin. Coll. Oxford; and jointly by CHARLES SANKEY, M.A. late Scholar of Queen's Coll. Oxford.

'The special purpose for which these manuals are intended, they will, we should think, admirably serve. Their clearness as narratives will make them acceptable to the schoolboy as well as to the teacher; and their critical acumen will commend them to the use of the more advanced student who is not only getting up, but trying to understand and appreciate, his HERODOTUS and THUCYDIDES. As for the general plan of the series of which they form part, we must confess, without wishing to draw comparisons for which we should be sorry to have to examine all the materials, that it strikes us as decidedly sensible. For the beginner, at all events, the most instructive, as it is the easiest and most natural, way of studying history is to study it by periods; and with regard to earlier Greek and Roman history at all events, there is no serious obstacle in the way of his being enabled to do so, since here period and what has come to be quasi-technically called subject frequently coincide, and form what may fairly be called an Epoch of Ancient History.' SATURDAY REVIEW.

The **GREEKS and the PERSIANS.** By the Rev. G. W. Cox, M.A. late Scholar of Trinity College, Oxford; Joint-Editor of the Series. With 4 Coloured Maps. Fcp. 8vo. price 2s. 6d.

The **EARLY ROMAN EMPIRE.** From the Assassination of Julius Cæsar to the Assassination of Domitian. By the Rev. W. WOLFE CAPES, M.A. Reader of Ancient History in the University of Oxford. With 2 Coloured Maps. Fcp. 8vo. price 2s. 6d.

ROME to its CAPTURE by the GAULS. By Wilhelm Ihne, Author of 'History of Rome.' With a Coloured Map. Fcp. 8vo. price 2s. 6d.

The **ATHENIAN EMPIRE from the FLIGHT of XERXES to the FALL** of ATHENS. By the Rev. G. W. Cox, M.A. late Scholar of Trinity College, Oxford; Joint-Editor of the Series. With 5 Maps. Fcp. 8vo. price 2s. 6d.

The **ROMAN TRIUMVIRATES.** By the Very Rev. Charles Merivale, D.D. Dean of Ely; Author of 'History of the Romans under the Empire.' With a Coloured Map. Fcp. 8vo. price 2s. 6d.

The **ROMAN EMPIRE of the SECOND CENTURY, or the AGE of the ANTONINES.** By the Rev. W. WOLFE CAPES, M.A. Reader of Ancient History in the University of Oxford. With 2 Coloured Maps. Fcp. 8vo. price 2s. 6d.

The **RISE of the MACEDONIAN EMPIRE.** By Arthur M. Curteis, M.A. formerly Fellow of Trinity College, Oxford, and late Assistant-Master in Sherborne School. With 8 Maps. Fcp. 8vo. price 2s. 6d.

The **GRACCHI, MARIUS, and SULLA.** By A. H. Beesly, M.A. Assistant-Master, Marlborough College. With 2 Maps. Fcp. 8vo. price 2s. 6d.

ROME and CARTHAGE, the PUNIC WARS. By R. Bosworth Smith, M.A. Assistant-Master, Harrow School. [*In the press.*

SPARTAN and THEBAN SUPREMACY. By Charles Sankey, M.A. late Scholar of Queen's College, Oxford; Assistant-Master, Marlborough College; Joint-Editor of the Series. [*In the press.*

London, LONGMANS & CO.

39 Paternoster Row, E.C.
London, *March* 1877.

GENERAL LIST OF WORKS

PUBLISHED BY

Messrs. Longmans, Green, & Co.

	PAGE		PAGE
Arts, Manufactures, &c.	15	Mental & Political Philosophy	5
Astronomy & Meteorology	10	Miscellaneous & Critical Works	7
Biographical Works	4	Natural History & Physical Science	11
Chemistry & Physiology	14	Poetry & the Drama	21
Dictionaries & other Books of Reference	8	Religious & Moral Works	16
Fine Arts & Illustrated Editions	14	Rural Sports, Horse & Cattle Management, &c.	18
History, Politics, Historical Memoirs, &c.	1	Travels, Voyages, &c.	19
Index	25 to 28	Works of Fiction	20
		Works of Utility & General Information	23

HISTORY, POLITICS, HISTORICAL MEMOIRS, &c.

Sketches of Ottoman History. By the Very Rev. R. W. Church, Dean of St. Paul's. 1 vol. crown 8vo. [*Nearly ready.*

The Eastern Question. By the Rev. Malcolm MacColl, M.A. 8vo. [*Nearly ready*].

The History of England from the Accession of James II. By the Right Hon. Lord Macaulay.
Student's Edition, 2 vols. cr. 8vo. 12*s.*
People's Edition, 4 vols. cr. 8vo. 16*s.*
Cabinet Edition, 8 vols. post 8vo. 48*s.*
Library Edition, 5 vols. 8vo. £4.

Critical and Historical Essays contributed to the Edinburgh Review. By the Right Hon. Lord Macaulay.
Cheap Edition, crown 8vo. 3*s.* 6*d.*
Student's Edition, crown 8vo. 6*s.*
People's Edition, 2 vols. crown 8vo. 8*s.*
Cabinet Edition, 4 vols. 24*s.*
Library Edition, 3 vols. 8vo. 36*s.*

Lord Macaulay's Works. Complete and uniform Library Edition. Edited by his Sister, Lady Trevelyan. 8 vols. 8vo. with Portrait, £5. 5*s.*

A

The History of England from the Fall of Wolsey to the Defeat of the Spanish Armada. By J. A. FROUDE, M.A.
CABINET EDITION, 12 vols. cr. 8vo. £3. 12s.
LIBRARY EDITION, 12 vols. 8vo. £8. 18s.

The English in Ireland in the Eighteenth Century. By J. A. FROUDE, M.A. 3 vols. 8vo. £2. 8s.

Journal of the Reigns of King George IV. and King William IV. By the late C. C. F. GREVILLE, Esq. Edited by H. REEVE, Esq. Fifth Edition. 3 vols. 8vo. price 36s.

The Life of Napoleon III. derived from State Records, Unpublished Family Correspondence, and Personal Testimony. By BLANCHARD JERROLD. In Four Volumes, 8vo. with numerous Portraits and Facsimiles. VOLS. I. and II. price 18s. each.
* The Third Volume is in the press.

Introductory Lectures on Modern History delivered in Lent Term 1842; with the Inaugural Lecture delivered in December 1841. By the late Rev. T. ARNOLD, D.D. 8vo. price 7s. 6d.

On Parliamentary Government in England; its Origin, Development, and Practical Operation. By ALPHEUS TODD. 2 vols. 8vo. price £1. 17s.

The Constitutional History of England since the Accession of George III. 1760-1870. By Sir THOMAS ERSKINE MAY, K.C.B. D.C.L. Fifth Edition. 3 vols. crown 8vo. 18s.

Democracy in Europe; a History. By Sir THOMAS ERSKINE MAY, K.C.B. D.C.L. 2 vols. 8vo.
[*In the press.*

History of Civilisation in England and France, Spain and Scotland. By HENRY THOMAS BUCKLE. 3 vols. crown 8vo. 24s.

Lectures on the History of England from the Earliest Times to the Death of King Edward II. By W. LONGMAN, F.S.A. Maps and Illustrations. 8vo. 15s.

History of the Life & Times of Edward III. By W. LONGMAN, F.S.A. With 9 Maps, 8 Plates, and 16 Woodcuts. 2 vols. 8vo. 28s.

The Life of Simon de Montfort, Earl of Leicester, with special reference to the Parliamentary History of his time. By GEORGE WALTER PROTHERO, Fellow and Lecturer in History, King's College, Cambridge. Crown 8vo. 9s.

History of England under the Duke of Buckingham and Charles the First, 1624-1628. By S. R. GARDINER, late Student of Ch. Ch. 2 vols. 8vo. with 2 Maps, 24s.

The Personal Government of Charles I. from the Death of Buckingham to the Declaration of the Judges in favour of Ship Money, 1628-1637. By S. R. GARDINER, late Student of Ch. Ch. 2 vols. 8vo.
[*In the press.*

Popular History of France, from the Earliest Times to the Death of Louis XIV. By ELIZABETH M. SEWELL. With 8 Maps. Crown 8vo. 7s. 6d.

History of Prussia, from the Earliest Times to the Present Day; tracing the Origin and Development of her Military Organisation. By Capt. W. J. WYATT. VOLS. I. & II. A.D. 700 to A.D. 1525. 8vo. 36s.

A Student's Manual of the History of India from the Earliest Period to the Present. By Col. MEADOWS TAYLOR, M.R.A.S. Second Thousand. Crown 8vo. Maps, 7s. 6d.

Indian Polity; a View of the System of Administration in India. By Lieut.-Col. G. CHESNEY. 2nd Edition, revised, with Map. 8vo. 21s.

Essays in Modern Military Biography. By Col. C. C. CHESNEY, R.E. 8vo. 12s. 6d.

Waterloo Lectures; a Study of the Campaign of 1815. By Col. C. C. Chesney, R.E. Third Edition. 8vo. Map, 10s. 6d.

The Oxford Reformers— John Colet, Erasmus, and Thomas More; being a History of their Fellow-Work. By F. Seebohm. Second Edition. 8vo. 14s.

The Mythology of the Aryan Nations. By the Rev. G. W. Cox, M.A. late Scholar of Trinity College, Oxford. 2 vols. 8vo. 28s.

A History of Greece. By the Rev. G. W. Cox, M.A. Vols. I. & II. 8vo. Maps, 36s.

General Hist. of Greece to the Death of Alexander the Great; with a Sketch of the Subsequent History to the Present Time. By the Rev. G. W. Cox, M.A. Crown 8vo. with Maps, 7s. 6d.

General History of Rome from the Foundation of the City to the Fall of Augustulus, B.C. 753-A.D. 476. By Dean Merivale, D.D. Crown 8vo. Maps, 7s. 6d.

History of the Romans under the Empire. By Dean Merivale, D.D. 8 vols. post 8vo. 48s.

The Fall of the Roman Republic; a Short History of the Last Century of the Commonwealth. By Dean Merivale, D.D. 12mo. 7s. 6d.

The History of Rome. By Wilhelm Ihne. Vols. I. & II. 8vo. 30s. Vol. III. is in the press.

The Sixth Oriental Monarchy; or, the Geography, History, and Antiquities of Parthia. By G. Rawlinson, M.A. With Maps and Illustrations. 8vo. 16s.

The Seventh Great Oriental Monarchy; or, a History of the Sassanians. By G. Rawlinson, M.A. With Map and 95 Illustrations. 8vo. 28s.

Encyclopædia of Chronology, Historical and Biographical; comprising the Dates of all the Great Events of History, including Treaties, Alliances, Wars, Battles, &c. By B. B. Woodward, B.A. and W. L. R. Cates. 8vo. 42s.

The History of European Morals from Augustus to Charlemagne. By W. E. H. Lecky, M.A. 2 vols. crown 8vo. 16s.

History of the Rise and Influence of the Spirit of Rationalism in Europe. By W. E. H. Lecky, M.A. 2 vols. crown 8vo. 16s.

The Native Races of the Pacific States of North America. By H. H. Bancroft. 5 vols. 8vo. £6. 5s.

History of the Mongols from the Ninth to the Nineteenth Century. By Henry H. Howorth, F.S.A. Vol. I. the Mongols Proper and the Kalmuks; with Two Coloured Maps. Royal 8vo. 28s.

Islam under the Arabs. By Robert Durie Osborn, Major in the Bengal Staff Corps. 8vo. 12s.

Introduction to the Science of Religion, Four Lectures delivered at the Royal Institution; with Two Essays on False Analogies and the Philosophy of Mythology. By Max Müller, M.A. Crown 8vo. 10s. 6d.

Zeller's Stoics, Epicureans, and Sceptics. Translated by the Rev. O. J. Reichel, M.A. Cr. 8vo. 14s.

Zeller's Socrates & the Socratic Schools. Translated by the Rev. O. J. Reichel, M.A. Crown 8vo. New Edition in the press.

Zeller's Plato & the Older Academy. Translated by S. Frances Alleyne and Alfred Goodwin, B.A. Crown 8vo. 18s.

Sketch of the History of the Church of England to the Revolution of 1688. By T. V. Short, D.D. sometime Bishop of St. Asaph. Crown 8vo. 7s. 6d.

NEW WORKS published by LONGMANS & CO.

The History of Philosophy, from Thales to Comte. By GEORGE HENRY LEWES. Fourth Edition. 2 vols. 8vo. 32s.

The Childhood of the English Nation; or, the Beginnings of English History. By ELLA S. ARMITAGE. Fcp. 8vo. 2s. 6d.

Epochs of Modern History. Edited by E. E. MORRIS, M.A. J. S. PHILLPOTTS, B.C.L. and C. COLBECK, M.A. Eleven volumes now published, each complete in itself, in fcp. 8vo. with Maps & Index :—

Cox's Crusades, 2s. 6d.
Creighton's Age of Elizabeth, 2s. 6d.
Gairdner's Houses of Lancaster and York, 2s. 6d.
Gardiner's Puritan Revolution, 2s. 6d.
Gardiner's Thirty Years' War, 2s. 6d.
Hale's Fall of the Stuarts, 2s. 6d.
Ludlow's War of American Independence, 2s. 6d.
Morris's Age of Anne, 2s. 6d.
Seebohm's Protestant Revolution, price 2s. 6d.
Stubbs's Early Plantagenets, 2s. 6d.
Warburton's Edward III. 2s. 6d.

* Other Epochs in preparation, in continuation of the Series.

The Student's Manual of Modern History; containing the Rise and Progress of the Principal European Nations. By W. COOKE TAYLOR, LL.D. Crown 8vo. 7s. 6d.

The Student's Manual of Ancient History; containing the Political History, Geographical Position, and Social State of the Principal Nations of Antiquity. By W. COOKE TAYLOR, LL.D. Crown 8vo. 7s. 6d.

Epochs of Ancient History. Edited by the Rev. G. W. COX, M.A. and by C. SANKEY, M.A. Ten volumes, each complete in itself, in fcp. 8vo. with Maps & Index :—

Beesly's Gracchi, Marius & Sulla, 2s. 6d.
Capes's Age of the Antonines, 2s. 6d.
Capes's Early Roman Empire, 2s. 6d.
Cox's Athenian Empire, 2s. 6d.
Cox's Greeks & Persians, 2s. 6d.
Curteis's Macedonian Empire, 2s. 6d.
Ihne's Rome to its Capture by the Gauls, 2s. 6d.
Merivale's Roman Triumvirates, 2s. 6d.
Sankey's Spartan & Theban Supremacy. [*In the press.*
Smith's Rome & Carthage, the Punic Wars. [*In the press.*

BIOGRAPHICAL WORKS.

The Life and Letters of Lord Macaulay. By his Nephew, G. OTTO TREVELYAN, M.P. Second Edition, with Additions and Corrections. 2 vols. 8vo. Portrait, 36s.

The Life of Sir William Fairbairn, Bart. F.R.S. Partly written by himself; edited and completed by W. POLE, F.R.S. 8vo. Portrait, 18s.

Arthur Schopenhauer, his Life and his Philosophy. By HELEN ZIMMERN. Post 8vo. Portrait, 7s. 6d.

The Life, Works, and Opinions of Heinrich Heine. By WILLIAM STIGAND. 2 vols. 8vo. Portrait, 28s.

The Life and Letters of Mozart. Translated from the German Biography of Dr. LUDWIG NOHL. by Lady WALLACE. 2 vols. post 8vo. with Two Portraits. [*Nearly ready.*

Felix Mendelssohn's Letters from Italy and Switzerland, and Letters from 1833 to 1847. Translated by Lady WALLACE. With Portrait. 2 vols. crown 8vo. 5s. each.

Life of Robert Frampton,
D.D. Bishop of Gloucester, deprived as a Non-Juror in 1689. Edited by T. S EVANS, M.A. Vicar of Shoreditch. Crown 8vo. Portrait, 10s. 6d.

Autobiography. By JOHN STUART MILL. 8vo. 7s. 6d.

Isaac Casaubon, 1559-1614. By MARK PATTISON, Rector of Lincoln College, Oxford. 8vo. 18s.

Biographical and Critical Essays. By A. HAYWARD, Q.C. Second Series, 2 vols. 8vo. 28s. Third Series, 1 vol. 8vo. 14s.

The Memoirs of Sir John Reresby, of Thrybergh, Bart. M.P. 1634-1689. Edited from the Original Manuscript by J. J. CARTWRIGHT, M.A. 8vo. 21s.

Leaders of Public Opinion in Ireland; Swift, Flood, Grattan, O'Connell. By W. E. H. LECKY, M.A. Crown 8vo. 7s. 6d.

Essays in Ecclesiastical Biography. By the Right Hon. Sir J. STEPHEN, LL.D. Crown 8vo. 7s. 6d.

Dictionary of General Biography; containing Concise Memoirs and Notices of the most Eminent Persons of all Ages and Countries. By W. L. R. CATES. 8vo. 25s.

Life of the Duke of Wellington. By the Rev. G. R. GLEIG, M.A. Crown 8vo. Portrait, 5s.

Memoirs of Sir Henry Havelock, K.C.B. By JOHN CLARK MARSHMAN. Crown 8vo. 3s. 6d.

Vicissitudes of Families. By Sir BERNARD BURKE, C.B. Two vols. crown 8vo. 21s.

Maunder's Biographical Treasury. Latest Edition, reconstructed and partly re-written, with above 1,600 additional Memoirs, by W. L. R. CATES. Fcp. 8vo. 6s.

MENTAL and POLITICAL PHILOSOPHY.

Comte's System of Positive Polity, or Treatise upon Sociology. Translated from the Paris Edition of 1851-1854, and furnished with Analytical Tables of Contents :—

VOL. I. **General View of Positivism** and Introductory Principles. Translated by J. H. BRIDGES, M.B., formerly Fellow of Oriel College, Oxford. 8vo. price 21s.

VOL. II. **The Social Statics,** or the Abstract Laws of Human Order. Translated by FREDERIC HARRISON, M.A. 8vo. price 14s.

VOL. III. **The Social Dynamics,** or the General Laws of Human Progress (the Philosophy of History). Translated by Professor BEESLY, M.A. 8vo. 21s.

VOL. IV. **The Synthesis of the Future of Mankind.** Translated by RICHARD CONGREVE, M.D. with an Appendix, containing Comte's Early Essays, translated by H. D. HUTTON, B.A. 8vo. [*Nearly ready.*]

Democracy in America. By ALEXIS DE TOCQUEVILLE. Translated by HENRY REEVE, Esq. Two vols. crown 8vo. 16s.

Essays, Critical and Biographical. By HENRY ROGERS. 2 vols. crown 8vo. 12s.

Essays on some Theological Controversies of the Time. By HENRY ROGERS. Crown 8vo. 6s.

On Representative Government. By JOHN STUART MILL. Crown 8vo. 2s.

On Liberty. By JOHN STUART MILL. Post 8vo. 7s. 6d. crown 8vo. 1s. 4d.

Principles of Political Economy. By JOHN STUART MILL. 2 vols. 8vo. 30s. or 1 vol. crown 8vo. 5s.

Essays on some Unsettled Questions of Political Economy. By JOHN STUART MILL. 8vo. 6s. 6d.

Utilitarianism. By JOHN STUART MILL. 8vo. 5s.

A System of Logic, Ratiocinative and Inductive. By JOHN STUART MILL. 2 vols. 8vo. 25s.

Examination of Sir William Hamilton's Philosophy, and of the principal Philosophical Questions discussed in his Writings. By JOHN STUART MILL. 8vo. 16s.

Dissertations and Discussions. By JOHN STUART MILL. 4 vols. 8vo. price £2. 6s. 6d.

Analysis of the Phenomena of the Human Mind. By JAMES MILL. With Notes, Illustrative and Critical. 2 vols. 8vo. 28s.

The Law of Nations considered as Independent Political Communities; the Rights and Duties of Nations in Time of War. By Sir TRAVERS TWISS, D.C.L. 8vo. 21s.

Church and State; their Relations Historically Developed. By H. GEFFCKEN, Prof. of International Law in the Univ. of Strasburg. Translated, with the Author's assistance, by E. F. TAYLOR. 2 vols. 8vo. 42s.

A Systematic View of the Science of Jurisprudence. By SHELDON AMOS, M.A. 8vo. 18s.

A Primer of the English Constitution and Government. By S. AMOS, M.A. Crown 8vo. 6s.

Outlines of Civil Procedure; a General View of the Supreme Court of Judicature and of the whole Practice in the Common Law and Chancery Divisions. By E. S. ROSCOE, Barrister-at-Law. 12mo. 3s. 6d.

A Sketch of the History of Taxes in England from the Earliest Times to the Present Day. By STEPHEN DOWELL. VOL. I. to the Civil War 1642. 8vo. 10s. 6d.

Principles of Economical Philosophy. By H. D. MACLEOD, M.A. Barrister-at-Law. Second Edition in Two Volumes. VOL. I. 8vo. 15s. VOL. II. PART I. price 12s.

The Institutes of Justinian; with English Introduction, Translation, and Notes. By T. C. SANDARS, M.A. 8vo. 18s.

Lord Bacon's Works, collected & edited by R. L. ELLIS, M.A. J. SPEDDING, M.A. and D. D. HEATH. 7 vols. 8vo. £3. 13s. 6d.

Letters and Life of Francis Bacon, including all his Occasional Works. Collected and edited, with a Commentary, by J. SPEDDING. 7 vols. 8vo. £4. 4s.

The Nicomachean Ethics of Aristotle, newly translated into English by R. WILLIAMS, B.A. Second Edition, thoroughly revised. Crown 8vo. 7s. 6d.

Aristotle's Politics, Books I. III. IV. (VII.) the Greek Text of Bekker, with an English Translation by W. E. BOLLAND, M.A. and Short Introductory Essays by A. LANG, M.A. Crown 8vo. 7s. 6d.

The Politics of Aristotle; Greek Text, with English Notes. By RICHARD CONGREVE, M.A. 8vo. 18s.

The Ethics of Aristotle; with Essays and Notes. By Sir A. GRANT, Bart. M.A. LL.D. 2 vols. 8vo. 32s.

Bacon's Essays, with Annotations. By R. WHATELY, D.D. 8vo. 10s. 6d.

Picture Logic; an Attempt to Popularise the Science of Reasoning. By A. SWINBOURNE, B.A. Fcp. 8vo. price 5s.

Elements of Logic. By R. WHATELY, D.D. 8vo. 10s. 6d. Crown 8vo. 4s. 6d.

Elements of Rhetoric. By R. WHATELY, D.D. 8vo. 10s. 6d. Crown 8vo. 4s. 6d.

An Introduction to Mental Philosophy, on the Inductive Method. By J. D. MORELL, LL.D. 8vo. 12s.

Philosophy without Assumptions. By the Rev. T. P. KIRKMAN, F.R.S. 8vo. 10s. 6d.

The Senses and the Intellect. By A. BAIN, LL.D. 8vo. 15s.

The Emotions and the Will. By A. BAIN, LL.D. 8vo. 15s.

Mental and Moral Science; a Compendium of Psychology and Ethics. By A. BAIN, LL.D. Crown 8vo. 10s. 6d. Or separately, PART I. Mental Science, 6s. 6d. PART II. Moral Science, 4s. 6d.

An Outline of the Necessary Laws of Thought: a Treatise on Pure and Applied Logic. By W. THOMPSON, D.D. Archbishop of York. Crown 8vo. 6s.

On the Influence of Authority in Matters of Opinion. By the late Sir. G. C. LEWIS, Bart. 8vo. 14s.

Hume's Treatise on Human Nature. Edited, with Notes, &c. by T. H. GREEN, M.A. and the Rev. T. H. GROSE, M.A. 2 vols. 8vo. 28s.

Hume's Essays, Moral, Political, and Literary. By the same Editors. 2 vols. 8vo. 28s.

*** The above form a complete and uniform Edition of HUME'S Philosophical Works.

MISCELLANEOUS & CRITICAL WORKS.

Selections from the Writings of Lord Macaulay. Edited, with Occasional Explanatory Notes, by G. O. TREVELYAN, M.P. Cr. 8vo. 6s.

Lord Macaulay's Miscellaneous Writings.
LIBRARY EDITION, 2 vols. 8vo. 21s.
PEOPLE'S EDITION, 1 vol. cr. 8vo. 4s. 6d.

Lord Macaulay's Miscellaneous Writings and Speeches. Student's Edition. Crown 8vo. 6s.

Speeches of the Right Hon. Lord Macaulay, corrected by Himself. Crown 8vo. 3s. 6d.

The Rev. Sydney Smith's Essays contributed to the Edinburgh Review. Crown 8vo. 2s. 6d. sewed, 3s. 6d. cloth.

The Wit and Wisdom of the Rev. Sydney Smith. Crown 8vo. 3s. 6d.

Miscellaneous and Posthumous Works of the late Henry Thomas Buckle. Edited, with a Biographical Notice, by HELEN TAYLOR. 3 vols. 8vo. £2. 12s. 6d.

Short Studies on Great Subjects. By J. A. FROUDE, M.A.
CABINET EDITION, 2 vols. crown 8vo. 12s.
LIBRARY EDITION, 2 vols. demy 8vo. 24s.
THIRD SERIES, in the press.

Manual of English Literature, Historical and Critical. By T. ARNOLD, M.A. Crown 8vo. 7s. 6d.

German Home Life; a Series of Essays on the Domestic Life of Germany. Crown 8vo. 6s.

Miscellaneous Works of Thomas Arnold, D.D. late Head Master of Rugby School. 8vo. 7s. 6d.

Realities of Irish Life. By W. STEUART TRENCH. Crown 8vo. 2s. 6d. sewed, or 3s. 6d. cloth.

B

Lectures on the Science of Language. By F. Max Müller, M.A. &c. 2 vols. crown 8vo. 16s.

Chips from a German Workshop; Essays on the Science of Religion, and on Mythology, Traditions & Customs. By F. Max Müller, M.A. 4 vols. 8vo. £2. 18s.

Chapters on Language. By F. W. Farrar, D.D. Crown 8vo. price 5s.

Families of Speech. Four Lectures delivered at the Royal Institution. By F. W. Farrar, D.D. Crown 8vo. 3s. 6d.

Apparitions; a Narrative of Facts. By the Rev. B. W. Savile, M.A. Crown 8vo. 4s. 6d.

Miscellaneous Writings of John Conington, M.A. Edited by J. A. Symonds, M.A. With a Memoir by H. J. S. Smith, M.A. 2 vols. 8vo. 28s.

The Essays and Contributions of A. K. H. B. Uniform Cabinet Editions in crown 8vo.

Recreations of a Country Parson, Two Series, 3s. 6d. each.

Landscapes, Churches, and Moralities, price 3s. 6d.

Seaside Musings, 3s. 6d.

Changed Aspects of Unchanged Truths, 3s. 6d.

Counsel and Comfort from a City Pulpit, 3s. 6d.

Lessons of Middle Age, 3s. 6d.

Leisure Hours in Town, 3s. 6d.

Autumn Holidays of a Country Parson, price 3s. 6d.

Sunday Afternoons at the Parish Church of a University City, 3s. 6d.

The Commonplace Philosopher in Town and Country, 3s. 6d.

Present-Day Thoughts, 3s. 6d.

Critical Essays of a Country Parson, price 3s. 6d.

The Graver Thoughts of a Country Parson, Three Series, 3s. 6d. each.

DICTIONARIES and OTHER BOOKS of REFERENCE.

Dictionary of the English Language. By R. G. Latham, M.A. M.D. Abridged from Dr. Latham's Edition of Johnson's English Dictionary. Medium 8vo. 24s.

A Dictionary of the English Language. By R. G. Latham, M.A. M.D. Founded on the Dictionary of Dr. S. Johnson, as edited by the Rev. H. J. Todd, with numerous Emendations and Additions. 4 vols. 4to. £7.

Thesaurus of English Words and Phrases, classified and arranged so as to facilitate the expression of Ideas, and assist in Literary Composition. By P. M. Roget, M.D. Crown 8vo. 10s. 6d.

English Synonymes. By E. J. Whately. Edited by R. Whately, D.D. Fcp. 8vo. 3s.

Handbook of the English Language. For the Use of Students of the Universities and the Higher Classes in Schools. By R. G. Latham, M.A. M.D. Crown 8vo. 6s.

A Practical Dictionary of the French and English Languages. By Léon Contanseau, many years French Examiner for Military and Civil Appointments, &c. Post 8vo. price 7s. 6d.

Contanseau's Pocket Dictionary, French and English, abridged from the Practical Dictionary by the Author. Square 18mo. 3s. 6d.

A New Pocket Dictionary of the German and English Languages. By F. W. Longman, Balliol College, Oxford. Square 18mo. price 5s.

A Practical Dictionary of the German Language; German-English and English-German. By Rev. W. L. Blackley, M.A. and Dr. C. M. Friedländer. Post 8vo. 7s. 6d.

A Dictionary of Roman and Greek Antiquities. With 2,000 Woodcuts Illustrative of the Arts and Life of the Greeks and Romans. By A. Rich, B.A. Crown 8vo. 7s. 6d.

A Greek-English Lexicon. By H. G. Liddell, D.D. Dean of Christchurch, and R. Scott, D.D. Dean of Rochester. Crown 4to. 36s.

A Lexicon, Greek and English, abridged for Schools from Liddell and Scott's Greek-English Lexicon. Square 12mo. 7s. 6d.

An English-Greek Lexicon, containing all the Greek Words used by Writers of good authority. By C. D. Yonge, M.A. 4to. 21s.

Mr. Yonge's Lexicon, English and Greek, abridged from his larger Lexicon. Square 12mo. 8s. 6d.

A Latin-English Dictionary. By John T. White, D.D. Oxon and J. E. Riddle, M.A. Oxon. Sixth Edition, revised. 1 vol. 4to. 28s.

White's College Latin-English Dictionary; abridged from the Parent Work for the use of University Students. Medium 8vo. 15s.

A Latin-English Dictionary adapted for the use of Middle-Class Schools. By John T. White, D.D. Oxon. Square fcp. 8vo. 3s.

White's Junior Student's Complete Latin-English and English-Latin Dictionary. Square 12mo. price 12s.

Separately { English-Latin, 5s. 6d.
{ Latin-English, 7s. 6d.

M'Culloch's Dictionary, Practical, Theoretical, and Historical, of Commerce and Commercial Navigation. Edited and corrected to 1876 by H. G. Reid. 8vo. 63s. Second Supplement, price 3s. 6d.

A General Dictionary of Geography, Descriptive, Physical, Statistical, and Historical; forming a complete Gazetteer of the World. By A. Keith Johnston. New Edition (1877), thoroughly revised. Medium 8vo. 42s.

Maunder's Treasury of Knowledge and Library of Reference; comprising an English Dictionary and Grammar, Universal Gazetteer, Classical Dictionary, Chronology, Law Dictionary, Synopsis of the Peerage, Useful Tables, &c. Fcp. 8vo. 6s.

The Treasury of Bible Knowledge; being a Dictionary of the Books, Persons, Places, Events, and other Matters of which mention is made in Holy Scripture. By the Rev. J. Ayre, M.A. With Maps, Plates, and many Woodcuts. Fcp. 8vo. 6s.

The Public Schools Atlas of Modern Geography. In 31 entirely new Coloured Maps. Edited with an Introduction by Rev. G. Butler, M.A. In imperial 8vo. or imperial 4to. price 5s. cloth.

The Public Schools Atlas of Ancient Geography, in 28 entirely new Coloured Maps. Edited with an Introduction by the Rev. G. Butler, M.A. In imperial 8vo. or imperial 4to. price 7s. 6d. cloth.

ASTRONOMY and METEOROLOGY.

The Universe and the Coming Transits; Researches into and New Views respecting the Constitution of the Heavens. By R. A. PROCTOR, B.A. With 22 Charts and 22 Diagrams. 8vo. 16s.

Saturn and its System. By R. A. PROCTOR, B.A. 8vo. with 14 Plates, 14s.

The Transits of Venus; A Popular Account of Past and Coming Transits. By R. A. PROCTOR, B.A. 20 Plates (12 Coloured) and 27 Woodcuts. Crown 8vo. 8s. 6d.

Essays on Astronomy. A Series of Papers on Planets and Meteors, the Sun and Sun-surrounding Space, Star and Star Cloudlets. By R. A. PROCTOR, B.A. With 10 Plates and 24 Woodcuts. 8vo. 12s.

The Moon; her Motions, Aspects, Scenery, and Physical Condition. By R. A. PROCTOR, B.A. With Plates, Charts, Woodcuts, and Lunar Photographs. Crown 8vo. 15s.

The Sun; Ruler, Light, Fire, and Life of the Planetary System. By R. A. PROCTOR, B.A. With Plates & Woodcuts. Crown 8vo. 14s.

The Orbs Around Us; a Series of Essays on the Moon & Planets, Meteors & Comets, the Sun & Coloured Pairs of Suns. By R. A. PROCTOR, B.A. With Chart and Diagrams. Crown 8vo. 7s. 6d.

Other Worlds than Ours; The Plurality of Worlds Studied under the Light of Recent Scientific Researches. By R. A. PROCTOR, B.A. With 14 Illustrations. Cr. 8vo. 10s. 6d.

Brinkley's Astronomy. Revised and partly re-written by JOHN W. STUBBS, D.D. and F. BRUNNOW, Ph.D. With 49 Diagrams. Crown 8vo. price 6s.

Outlines of Astronomy. By Sir J. F. W. HERSCHEL, Bart. M.A. Latest Edition, with Plates and Diagrams. Square crown 8vo. 12s.

The Moon, and the Condition and Configurations of its Surface. By E. NEISON, F.R. Ast. Soc. &c. With 26 Maps and 5 Plates. Medium 8vo. 31s. 6d.

Celestial Objects for Common Telescopes. By T. W. WEBB, M.A. With Map of the Moon and Woodcuts. Crown 8vo. 7s. 6d.

A New Star Atlas, for the Library, the School, and the Observatory, in 12 Circular Maps (with 2 Index Plates). By R. A. PROCTOR, B.A. Crown 8vo. 5s.

Larger Star Atlas, for the Library, in Twelve Circular Maps, photolithographed by A. Brothers, F.R.A.S. With 2 Index Plates and a Letterpress Introduction. By R. A. PROCTOR, B.A. Small folio, 25s.

Dove's Law of Storms, considered in connexion with the Ordinary Movements of the Atmosphere. Translated by R. H. SCOTT, M.A. 8vo. 10s. 6d.

Air and Rain; the Beginnings of a Chemical Climatology. By R. A. SMITH, F.R.S. 8vo. 24s.

Air and its Relations to Life, 1774-1874; a Course of Lectures delivered at the Royal Institution of Great Britain. By W. N. HARTLEY, F.C.S. With 66 Woodcuts. Small 8vo. 6s.

Schellen's Spectrum Analysis, in its Application to Terrestrial Substances and the Physical Constitution of the Heavenly Bodies. Translated by JANE and C. LASSELL, with Notes by W. HUGGINS, LL.D. F.R.S. 8vo. Plates and Woodcuts, 28s.

NATURAL HISTORY and PHYSICAL SCIENCE.

**Professor Helmholtz'
Popular Lectures on Scientific Subjects.** Translated by E. Atkinson, F.C.S. With numerous Wood Engravings. 8vo. 12s. 6d.

On the Sensations of Tone, as a Physiological Basis for the Theory of Music. By H. Helmholtz, Professor of Physiology in the University of Berlin. Translated by A. J. Ellis, F.R.S. 8vo. 36s.

Ganot's Natural Philosophy for General Readers and Young Persons; a Course of Physics divested of Mathematical Formulæ and expressed in the language of daily life. Translated by E. Atkinson, F.C.S. Second Edition, with 2 Plates and 429 Woodcuts. Crown 8vo. 7s. 6d.

Ganot's Elementary Treatise on Physics, Experimental and Applied, for the use of Colleges and Schools. Translated and edited by E. Atkinson, F.C.S. Seventh Edition, with 4 Coloured Plates and 758 Woodcuts. Post 8vo. 15s.

Arnott's Elements of Physics or Natural Philosophy. Seventh Edition, edited by A. Bain, LL.D. and A. S. Taylor, M.D. F.R.S. Crown 8vo. Woodcuts, 12s. 6d.

The Correlation of Physical Forces. By the Hon. Sir W. R. Grove, F.R.S. &c. Sixth Edition, with other Contributions to Science. 8vo. 15s.

Weinhold's Introduction to Experimental Physics; including Directions for Constructing Physical Apparatus and for Making Experiments. Translated by B. Loewy, F.R.A.S. With a Preface by G. C. Foster, F.R.S. 8vo. Plates & Woodcuts 31s. 6d.

Principles of Animal Mechanics. By the Rev. S. Haughton, F.R.S. Second Edition. 8vo. 21s.

Fragments of Science. By John Tyndall, F.R.S. Fifth Edition, with a New Introduction. Crown 8vo. 10s. 6d.

Heat a Mode of Motion. By John Tyndall, F.R.S. Fifth Edition, Plate and Woodcuts. Crown 8vo. 10s. 6d.

Sound. By John Tyndall, F.R.S. Third Edition, including Recent Researches on Fog Signalling ; Portrait and Woodcuts. Crown 8vo. price 10s. 6d.

Researches on Diamagnetism and Magne-Crystallic Action; including Diamagnetic Polarity. By John Tyndall, F.R.S. With 6 Plates and many Woodcuts. 8vo. 14s.

Contributions to Molecular Physics in the domain of Radiant Heat. By John Tyndall, F.R.S. With 2 Plates and 31 Woodcuts. 8vo. 16s.

Six Lectures on Light, delivered in America in 1872 and 1873. By John Tyndall, F.R.S. Second Edition, with Portrait, Plate, and 59 Diagrams. Crown 8vo. 7s. 6d.

Notes of a Course of Nine Lectures on Light, delivered at the Royal Institution. By John Tyndall, F.R.S. Crown 8vo. 1s. sewed, or 1s. 6d. cloth.

Notes of a Course of Seven Lectures on Electrical Phenomena and Theories, delivered at the Royal Institution. By John Tyndall, F.R.S. Crown 8vo. 1s. sewed, or 1s. 6d. cloth.

A Treatise on Magnetism, General and Terrestrial. By H. Lloyd, D.D. D.C.L. 8vo. 10s. 6d.

Elementary Treatise on the Wave-Theory of Light. By H. Lloyd, D.D. D.C.L. 8vo. 10s. 6d.

Text-Books of Science,

Mechanical and Physical, adapted for the use of Artisans and of Students in Public and Science Schools. Small 8vo. with Woodcuts, &c.

Anderson's Strength of Materials, 3s. 6d.
Armstrong's Organic Chemistry, 3s. 6d.
Barry's Railway Appliances, 3s. 6d.
Bloxam's Metals, 3s. 6d.
Goodeve's Mechanics, 3s. 6d.
——— Mechanism, 3s. 6d.
Griffin's Algebra & Trigonometry, 3/6.
Jenkin's Electricity & Magnetism, 3/6.
Maxwell's Theory of Heat, 3s. 6d.
Merrifield's Technical Arithmetic, 3s. 6d.
Miller's Inorganic Chemistry, 3s. 6d.
Preece & Sivewright's Telegraphy, 3/6.
Shelley's Workshop Appliances, 3s 6d.
Thomé's Structural and Physiological Botany, 6s.
Thorpe's Quantitative Analysis, 4s. 6d.
Thorpe & Muir's Qualitative Analysis, price 3s. 6d.
Tilden's Systematic Chemistry, 3s. 6d.
Unwin's Machine Design, 3s. 6d.
Watson's Plane & Solid Geometry, 3/6.

⁎ Other Text-Books, in continuation of this Series, in active preparation.

The Comparative Anatomy and Physiology of the Vertebrate Animals. By RICHARD OWEN, F.R.S. With 1,472 Woodcuts. 3 vols. 8vo. £3. 13s. 6d.

Kirby and Spence's Introduction to Entomology, or Elements of the Natural History of Insects. Crown 8vo. 5s.

Light Science for Leisure Hours; Familiar Essays on Scientific Subjects, Natural Phenomena, &c. By R. A. PROCTOR, B.A. 2 vols. crown 8vo. 7s. 6d. each.

Homes without Hands; a Description of the Habitations of Animals, classed according to their Principle of Construction. By the Rev. J. G. WOOD, M.A. With about 140 Vignettes on Wood. 8vo. 14s.

Strange Dwellings; a Description of the Habitations of Animals, abridged from 'Homes without Hands.' By the Rev. J. G. WOOD, M.A. With Frontispiece and 60 Woodcuts. Crown 8vo. 7s. 6d

Insects at Home; a Popular Account of British Insects, their Structure, Habits, and Transformations. By the Rev. J. G. WOOD, M.A. With upwards of 700 Woodcuts. 8vo. price 14s.

Insects Abroad; being a Popular Account of Foreign Insects, their Structure, Habits, and Transformations. By the Rev. J. G. WOOD, M.A. With upwards of 700 Woodcuts. 8vo. 14s.

Out of Doors; a Selection of Original Articles on Practical Natural History. By the Rev. J. G. WOOD, M.A. With 6 Illustrations. Crown 8vo. 7s. 6d.

Bible Animals; a Description of every Living Creature mentioned in the Scriptures, from the Ape to the Coral. By the Rev. J. G. WOOD, M.A. With 112 Vignettes. 8vo. 14s.

The Polar World: a Popular Description of Man and Nature in the Arctic and Antarctic Regions of the Globe. By Dr. G. HARTWIG. With Chromoxylographs, Maps, and Woodcuts. 8vo. 10s. 6d.

The Sea and its Living Wonders. By Dr. G. HARTWIG. Fourth Edition, enlarged. 8vo. with numerous Illustrations, 10s. 6d.

The Tropical World. By Dr. G. HARTWIG. With about 200 Illustrations. 8vo. 10s. 6d.

The Subterranean World. By Dr. G. HARTWIG. With Maps and Woodcuts. 8vo. 10s. 6d.

The Aerial World; a Popular Account of the Phenomena and Life of the Atmosphere. By Dr. G. HARTWIG. With Map, 8 Chromoxylographs & 60 Woodcuts. 8vo. 21s.

Maunder's Treasury of Natural History, or Popular Dictionary of Animated Nature; in which the Zoological Characteristics that distinguish the different Classes, Genera and Species, are combined with a variety of interesting Information illustrative of the Habits, Instincts, and General Economy of the Animal Kingdom. Fcp. 8vo. with 900 Woodcuts, 6s.

A Familiar History of Birds. By E. Stanley, D.D. late Bishop of Norwich. Fcp. 8vo. with Woodcuts, 3s. 6d.

Rocks Classified and Described. By B. Von Cotta. English Edition by P. H. Lawrence (with English, German, and French Synonymes); revised by the Author. Post 8vo. 14s.

The Geology of England and Wales; a Concise Account of the Lithological Characters, Leading Fossils, and Economic Products of the Rocks. By H. B. Woodward, F.G.S. Crown 8vo. Map & Woodcuts, 14s.

The Primæval World of Switzerland. By Professor Oswald Heer, of the University of Zurich. Edited by James Heywood, M.A. F.R.S. President of the Statistical Society. With Map, 19 Plates, & 372 Woodcuts. 2 vols. 8vo. 28s.

The Puzzle of Life and How it Has Been Put Together: a Short History of Vegetable and Animal Life upon the Earth from the Earliest Times; including an Account of Pre-Historic Man, his Weapons, Tools, and Works. By A. Nicols, F.R.G.S. With 12 Illustrations. Crown 8vo. 5s.

The Origin of Civilisation, and the Primitive Condition of Man; Mental and Social Condition of Savages. By Sir J. Lubbock, Bart. M.P. F.R.S. Third Edition, with 25 Woodcuts. 8vo. 18s.

The Ancient Stone Implements, Weapons, and Ornaments of Great Britain. By John Evans, F.R.S. With 2 Plates and 476 Woodcuts. 8vo. 28s.

The Elements of Botany for Families and Schools. Eleventh Edition, revised by Thomas Moore, F.L.S. Fcp. 8vo. Woodcuts, 2s. 6d.

The Rose Amateur's Guide. By Thomas Rivers. Latest Edition. Fcp. 8vo. 4s.

A Dictionary of Science, Literature, and Art. Re-edited by the late W. T. Brande (the Author) and the Rev. G. W. Cox, M.A. 3 vols. medium 8vo. 63s.

The History of Modern Music, a Course of Lectures delivered at the Royal Institution of Great Britain. By John Hullah. Second Edition. Demy 8vo. 8s. 6d.

Mr. Hullah's 2nd Course of Lectures on the Transition Period of Musical History, from the Beginning of the Seventeenth to the Middle of the Eighteenth Century. Second Edition. Demy 8vo. 10s. 6d.

Structural and Physiological Botany. By Otto W. Thomé, Professor of Botany at the School of Science and Art, Cologne. Translated and edited by A. W. Bennett, M.A. B.Sc. F.L.S. Lecturer on Botany at St. Thomas's Hospital. With about 600 Woodcuts and a Coloured Map. Small 8vo. 6s.

The Treasury of Botany, or Popular Dictionary of the Vegetable Kingdom; with which is incorporated a Glossary of Botanical Terms. Edited by J. Lindley, F.R.S. and T. Moore, F.L.S. With 274 Woodcuts and 20 Steel Plates. Two Parts, fcp. 8vo. 12s.

Loudon's Encyclopædia of Plants; comprising the Specific Character, Description, Culture, History, &c. of all the Plants found in Great Britain. With upwards of 12,000 Woodcuts. 8vo. 42s.

De Caisne & Le Maout's
System of Descriptive and Analytical Botany. Translated by Mrs. HOOKER; edited and arranged according to the English Botanical System, by J. D. HOOKER, M.D. With 5,500 Woodcuts. Imperial 8vo. 31s. 6d.

Hand-Book of Hardy
Trees, Shrubs, and Herbaceous Plants; containing Descriptions &c. of the Best Species in Cultivation. With 720 Original Woodcut Illustrations. By W. B. HEMSLEY. Medium 8vo. 12s.

CHEMISTRY and PHYSIOLOGY.

Miller's Elements of Chemistry,
Theoretical and Practical. Re-edited, with Additions, by H. MACLEOD, F.C.S. 3 vols. 8vo.
PART I. CHEMICAL PHYSICS, New Edition in the press.
PART II. INORGANIC CHEMISTRY, 21s.
PART III. ORGANIC CHEMISTRY, New Edition in the press.

Health in the House:
Twenty-five Lectures on Elementary Physiology in its Application to the Daily Wants of Man and Animals. By Mrs. C. M. BUCKTON. Crown 8vo. Woodcuts, 2s.

Outlines of Physiology,
Human and Comparative. By J. MARSHALL, F.R.C.S. Surgeon to the University College Hospital. 2 vols. crown 8vo. with 122 Woodcuts, 32s.

An Introduction to the
Study of Chemical Philosophy; or, the Principles of Theoretical and Systematic Chemistry. By W. A. TILDEN, F.C.S. Small 8vo. 3s. 6d.

Select Methods in Chemical Analysis,
chiefly Inorganic. By WM. CROOKES, F.R.S. With 22 Woodcuts. Crown 8vo. 12s. 6d.

A Dictionary of Chemistry and the Allied Branches of other Sciences.
By HENRY WATTS, F.C.S. assisted by eminent Scientific and Practical Chemists. 7 vols. medium 8vo. £10. 16s. 6d.

Supplementary Volume,
completing the Record of Chemical Discovery to the year 1876.
[*In preparation.*

The FINE ARTS and ILLUSTRATED EDITIONS.

Poems. By W. B. SCOTT.
Illustrated by Seventeen Etchings by L. A. TADEMA and W. B. SCOTT. Crown 8vo. 15s.

Half-hour Lectures on
the History and Practice of the Fine and Ornamental Arts. By W. B. SCOTT. Cr. 8vo. Woodcuts, 8s. 6d.

A Dictionary of Artists of
the English School: Painters, Sculptors, Architects, Engravers, and Ornamentists. By S. REDGRAVE. 8vo. 16s.

In Fairyland; Pictures
from the Elf-World. By RICHARD DOYLE. With a Poem by W. ALLINGHAM. With 16 coloured Plates, containing 36 Designs. Folio, 15s.

Lord Macaulay's Lays of
Ancient Rome. With 90 Illustrations on Wood from Drawings by G. SCHARF. Fcp. 4to. 21s.

Miniature Edition, with
G. Scharf's 90 Illustrations reduced in Lithography. Imp. 16mo. 10s. 6d.

NEW WORKS published by LONGMANS & CO.   15

Moore's Lalla Rookh, Tenniel's Edition, with 68 Wood Engravings from Original Drawings. Fcp. 4to. 21s.

Moore's Irish Melodies, Maclise's Edition, with 161 Steel Plates. Super royal 8vo. 21s.

The New Testament, Illustrated with Wood Engravings after the Early Masters, chiefly of the Italian School. Crown 4to. 63s.

Sacred and Legendary Art. By Mrs. Jameson. 6 vols. square crown 8vo. price £5. 15s. 6d.

Legends of the Saints and Martyrs. With 19 Etchings and 187 Woodcuts. 2 vols. 31s. 6d.

Legends of the Monastic Orders. With 11 Etchings and 88 Woodcuts. 1 vol. 21s.

Legends of the Madonna. With 27 Etchings and 165 Woodcuts. 1 vol. 21s.

The History of our Lord, with that of his Types and Precursors. Completed by Lady Eastlake. With 13 Etchings and 281 Woodcuts. 2 vols. 42s.

The Three Cathedrals dedicated to St. Paul in London; their History from the Foundation of the First Building in the Sixth Century to the Proposals for the Adornment of the Present Cathedral. By W. Longman, F.S.A. With numerous Illustrations. Square crown 8vo. 21s.

The USEFUL ARTS, MANUFACTURES, &c.

The Amateur Mechanics' Practical Handbook; describing the different Tools required in the Workshop, the uses of them, and how to use them. By A. H. G. Hobson. With 33 Woodcuts. Crown 8vo. 2s. 6d.

The Engineer's Valuing Assistant. By H. D. Hoskold, Civil and Mining Engineer, 16 years Mining Engineer to the Dean Forest Iron Company. 8vo. [In the press.

The Whitworth Measuring Machine; including Descriptions of the Surface Plates, Gauges, and other Measuring Instruments made by Sir J. Whitworth, Bart. By T. M. Goodeve, M.A. and C. P. B. Shelley, C.E. Fcp. 4to. with 4 Plates and 44 Woodcuts. [Nearly ready.

Industrial Chemistry; a Manual for Manufacturers and for Colleges or Technical Schools; a Translation of Stohmann and Engler's German Edition of Payen's 'Précis de Chimie Industrielle,' by Dr. J. D. Barry. With Chapters on the Chemistry of the Metals, by B. H. Paul, Ph.D. 8vo. Plates & Woodcuts. [In the press.

Gwilt's Encyclopædia of Architecture, with above 1,600 Woodcuts. Revised and extended by W. Papworth. 8vo. 52s. 6d.

Lathes and Turning, Simple, Mechanical, and Ornamental. By W. H. Northcott. Second Edition, with 338 Illustrations. 8vo. 18s.

Hints on Household Taste in Furniture, Upholstery, and other Details. By C. L. Eastlake. With about 90 Illustrations. Square crown 8vo. 14s.

Handbook of Practical Telegraphy. By R. S. Culley, Memb. Inst. C.E. Engineer-in-Chief of Telegraphs to the Post-Office. 8vo. Plates & Woodcuts. 16s.

A Treatise on the Steam Engine, in its various applications to Mines, Mills, Steam Navigation, Railways and Agriculture. By J. Bourne, C.E. With Portrait, 37 Plates, and 546 Woodcuts. 4to. 42s.

Recent Improvements in the Steam Engine. By J. Bourne, C.E. Fcp. 8vo. Woodcuts. 6s.

C

Catechism of the Steam
Engine, in its various Applications. By JOHN BOURNE, C.E. Fcp. 8vo. Woodcuts, 6s.

Handbook of the Steam
Engine By J. BOURNE, C.E. forming a Key to the Author's Catechism of the Steam Engine. Fcp. 8vo. Woodcuts, 9s.

Encyclopædia of Civil
Engineering, Historical, Theoretical, and Practical. By E. CRESY, C.E. With above 3,000 Woodcuts. 8vo. 42s.

Ure's Dictionary of Arts,
Manufactures, and Mines. Seventh Edition, re-written and enlarged by R. HUNT, F.R.S. assisted by numerous contributors. With 2,100 Woodcuts. 3 vols. medium 8vo. £5. 5s.

VOL. IV. Supplementary, completing all the Departments of the Dictionary to the beginning of the year 1877, is preparing for publication.

Practical Treatise on Metallurgy.
Adapted from the last German Edition of Professor KERL'S Metallurgy by W. CROOKES, F.R.S. &c. and E. RÖHRIG, Ph.D. 3 vols. 8vo. with 625 Woodcuts. £4. 19s.

The Theory of Strains in
Girders and similar Structures, with Observations on the application of Theory to Practice, and Tables of the Strength and other Properties of Materials. By B. B. STONEY, M.A. M. Inst. C.E. Royal 8vo. with 5 Plates and 123 Woodcuts, 36s.

Treatise on Mills and
Millwork. By Sir W. FAIRBAIRN, Bt. With 18 Plates and 322 Woodcuts. 2 vols. 8vo. 32s.

Useful Information for
Engineers. By Sir W. FAIRBAIRN, Bt. With many Plates and Woodcuts. 3 vols. crown 8vo. 31s. 6d.

The Application of Cast
and Wrought Iron to Building Purposes. By Sir W. FAIRBAIRN, Bt. With 6 Plates and 118 Woodcuts. 8vo. 16s.

Practical Handbook of
Dyeing and Calico-Printing. By W. CROOKES, F.R.S. &c. With numerous Illustrations and specimens of Dyed Textile Fabrics. 8vo. 42s.

Anthracen; its Constitution,
Properties, Manufacture, and Derivatives, including Artificial Alizarin, Anthrapurpurin, &c. with their Applications in Dyeing and Printing. By G. AUERBACH. Translated by W. CROOKES, F.R.S. 8vo. 12s.

Mitchell's Manual of
Practical Assaying. Fourth Edition, revised, with the Recent Discoveries incorporated, by W. CROOKES, F.R.S. Crown 8vo. Woodcuts, 31s. 6d.

Loudon's Encyclopædia
of Gardening; comprising the Theory and Practice of Horticulture, Floriculture, Arboriculture, and Landscape Gardening. With 1,000 Woodcuts. 8vo. 21s.

Loudon's Encyclopædia
of Agriculture; comprising the Laying-out, Improvement, and Management of Landed Property, and the Cultivation and Economy of the Productions of Agriculture. With 1,100 Woodcuts. 8vo. 21s.

RELIGIOUS and MORAL WORKS.

An Exposition of the 39
Articles, Historical and Doctrinal. By E. H. BROWNE, D.D. Bishop of Winchester. Latest Edition. 8vo. 16s.

An Introduction to the
Theology of the Church of England, in an Exposition of the 39 Articles. By T. P. BOULTBEE, LL.D. Fcp. 8vo. 6s.

Historical Lectures on the Life of Our Lord Jesus Christ. By C. J. ELLICOTT, D.D. 8vo. 12s.

Sermons Chiefly on the Interpretation of Scripture. By the late Rev. THOMAS ARNOLD, D.D. 8vo. 7s. 6d.

Sermons preached in the Chapel of Rugby School; with an Address before Confirmation. By THOMAS ARNOLD, D.D. Fcp. 8vo. price 3s. 6d.

Christian Life, its Course, its Hindrances, and its Helps; Sermons preached mostly in the Chapel of Rugby School. By THOMAS ARNOLD, D.D. 8vo. 7s. 6d.

Christian Life, its Hopes, its Fears, and its Close; Sermons preached mostly in the Chapel of Rugby School. By THOMAS ARNOLD, D.D. 8vo. 7s. 6d.

Synonyms of the Old Testament, their Bearing on Christian Faith and Practice. By the Rev. R. B. GIRDLESTONE. 8vo. 15s.

The Primitive and Catholic Faith in Relation to the Church of England. By the Rev. B. W. SAVILE, M.A. 8vo. 7s.

The Eclipse of Faith; or a Visit to a Religious Sceptic. By HENRY ROGERS. Latest Edition. Fcp. 8vo. 5s.

Defence of the Eclipse of Faith. By HENRY ROGERS. Latest Edition. Fcp. 8vo. 3s. 6d.

Three Essays on Religion: Nature; the Utility of Religion; Theism. By JOHN STUART MILL. 8vo. 10s. 6d.

A Critical and Grammatical Commentary on St. Paul's Epistles. By C. J. ELLICOTT, D.D. 8vo. Galatians, 8s. 6d. Ephesians, 8s. 6d. Pastoral Epistles, 10s. 6d. Philippians, Colossians, & Philemon, 10s. 6d. Thessalonians, 7s. 6d.

The Life and Epistles of St. Paul. By Rev. W. J. CONYBEARE, M.A. and Very Rev. JOHN SAUL HOWSON, D.D. Dean of Chester. Three Editions, copiously illustrated.

Library Edition, with all the Original Illustrations, Maps, Landscapes on Steel, Woodcuts, &c. 2 vols. 4to. 42s.

Intermediate Edition, with a Selection of Maps, Plates, and Woodcuts. 2 vols. square crown 8vo. 21s.

Student's Edition, revised and condensed, with 46 Illustrations and Maps. 1 vol. crown 8vo. 9s.

Evidence of the Truth of the Christian Religion derived from the Literal Fulfilment of Prophecy. By ALEXANDER KEITH, D.D. 40th Edition, with numerous Plates. Square 8vo. 12s. 6d. or in post 8vo. with 5 Plates, 6s.

The Prophets and Prophecy in Israel; an Historical and Critical Inquiry. By Dr. A. KUENEN, Prof. of Theol. in the Univ. of Leyden. Translated from the Dutch by the Rev. A. MILROY, M.A. with an Introduction by J. MUIR, D.C.L. 8vo. 21s.

Mythology among the Hebrews and its Historical Development. By IGNAZ GOLDZIHER, Ph.D. Translated by RUSSELL MARTINEAU, M.A. 8vo. 16s.

Historical and Critical Commentary on the Old Testament; with a New Translation. By M. M. KALISCH, Ph.D. Vol. I. Genesis, 8vo. 18s. or adapted for the General Reader, 12s. Vol. II. Exodus, 15s. or adapted for the General Reader, 12s. Vol. III. Leviticus, Part I. 15s. or adapted for the General Reader, 8s. Vol. IV. Leviticus, Part II. 15s. or adapted for the General Reader, 8s.

The History and Literature of the Israelites, according to the Old Testament and the Apocrypha. By C. DE ROTHSCHILD & A. DE ROTHSCHILD. 2 vols. crown 8vo. 12s. 6d. Abridged Edition, 1 vol. fcp. 8vo. 3s. 6d.

Ewald's History of Israel. Translated from the German by J. E. CARPENTER, M.A. with Preface by R. MARTINEAU, M.A. 5 vols. 8vo. 63s.

Ewald's Antiquities of Israel. Translated from the German by H. S. SOLLY, M.A. 8vo. 12s. 6d.

Behind the Veil; an Outline of Bible Metaphysics compared with Ancient and Modern Thought. By the Rev. T. GRIFFITH, M.A. Prebendary of St. Paul's. 8vo. 10s. 6d.

The Trident, the Crescent & the Cross; a View of the Religious History of India during the Hindu, Buddhist, Mohammedan, and Christian Periods. By the Rev. J. VAUGHAN, Nineteen Years Missionary in India. 8vo. 9s. 6d.

The Types of Genesis, briefly considered as revealing the Development of Human Nature. By ANDREW JUKES. Crown 8vo. 7s. 6d.

The Second Death and the Restitution of all Things; with some Preliminary Remarks on the Nature and Inspiration of Holy Scripture. By A. JUKES. Crown 8vo. 3s. 6d.

History of the Reformation in Europe in the time of Calvin. By the Rev. J. H. MERLE D'AUBIGNÉ, D.D. Translated by W. L. R. CATES. 7 vols. 8vo. price £5. 11s.

VOL. VIII. translated by W. L. R. CATES, and completing the English Edition of Dr. D'AUBIGNÉ's Work, is in the press.

Supernatural Religion; an Inquiry into the Reality of Divine Revelation. 2 vols. 8vo. 24s.

Commentaries, by the Rev. W. A. O'CONOR, B.A. Rector of St. Simon and St. Jude, Manchester.
Epistle to the Romans, crown 8vo. 3s. 6d.
Epistle to the Hebrews, 4s. 6d.
St. John's Gospel, 10s. 6d.

An Introduction to the Study of the New Testament, Exegetical, and Theological. By the Rev. S. DAVIDSON, D.D. L.L.D. 2 vols. 8vo. 30s.

Passing Thoughts on Religion. By ELIZABETH M. SEWELL. Fcp. 8vo. 3s. 6d.

Thoughts for the Age. by ELIZABETH M. SEWELL. New Edition. Fcp. 8vo. 3s. 6d.

Some Questions of the Day. By ELIZABETH M. SEWELL. Crown 8vo. 2s. 6d.

Self-examination before Confirmation. By ELIZABETH M. SEWELL. 32mo. 1s. 6d.

Preparation for the Holy Communion; the Devotions chiefly from the works of Jeremy Taylor. By ELIZABETH M. SEWELL. 32mo. 3s.

Bishop Jeremy Taylor's Entire Works; with Life by Bishop Heber. Revised and corrected by the Rev. C. P. EDEN. 10 vols. £5. 5s.

Hymns of Praise and Prayer. Corrected and edited by Rev. JOHN MARTINEAU, LL.D. Crown 8vo. 4s. 6d. 32mo. 1s. 6d.

Spiritual Songs for the Sundays and Holidays throughout the Year. By J. S. B. MONSELL, LL.D. Fcp. 8vo. 5s. 18mo. 2s.

Lyra Germanica; Hymns translated from the German by Miss C. WINKWORTH. Fcp. 8vo. 5s.

Hours of Thought on Sacred Things; a Volume of Sermons. By JAMES MARTINEAU, D.D. LL.D. Crown 8vo. Price 7s. 6d.

Endeavours after the Christian Life; Discourses. By JAMES MARTINEAU, D.D. LL.D. Fifth Edition. Crown 8vo. 7s. 6d.

The Pentateuch & Book of Joshua Critically Examined. By J. W. COLENSO, D.D. Bishop of Natal. Crown 8vo. 6s.

Lectures on the Penta- teuch and the Moabite Stone; with Appendices. By J. W. COLENSO, D.D. Bishop of Natal. 8vo. 12s.

TRAVELS, VOYAGES, &c.

A Year in Western France. By M. BETHAM-EDWARDS. Crown 8vo. Frontispiece, 10s. 6d.

Journal of a Residence in Vienna and Berlin during the eventful Winter 1805-6. By the late HENRY REEVE, M.D. Published by his Son. Crown 8vo. 8s. 6d.

One Thousand Miles up the Nile; a Journey through Egypt and Nubia to the Second Cataract. By AMELIA B. EDWARDS. With Facsimiles of Inscriptions, Ground Plans, Two Coloured Maps, and 80 Illustrations engraved on Wood from Drawings by the Author. Imperial 8vo. 42s.

The Indian Alps, and How we Crossed them: a Narrative of Two Years' Residence in the Eastern Himalayas, and Two Months' Tour into the Interior. By a Lady Pioneer. With Illustrations from Original Drawings by the Author. Imperial 8vo. 42s.

Discoveries at Ephesus, Including the Site and Remains of the Great Temple of Diana. By J. T. WOOD, F.S.A. With 27 Lithographic Plates and 42 Wood Engravings. Medium 8vo. 63s.

Through Bosnia and the Herzegovina on Foot during the Insurrection, August and September 1875. By ARTHUR J. EVANS, B.A. F.S.A. Second Edition. Map & Illustrations. 8vo. 18s.

Italian Alps; Sketches in the Mountains of Ticino, Lombardy, the Trentino, and Venetia. By DOUGLAS W. FRESHFIELD. Square crown 8vo. Illustrations, 15s.

Over the Sea and Far Away; a Narrative of a Ramble round the World. By T. W. HINCHLIFF, M.A. F.R.G.S. President of the Alpine Club. With 14 full-page Illustrations engraved on Wood. Medium 8vo. 21s.

The Frosty Caucasus; an Account of a Walk through Part of the Range, and of an Ascent of Elbruz in the Summer of 1874. By F. C. GROVE. With Eight Illustrations and a Map. Crown 8vo. price 15s.

Tyrol and the Tyrolese; an Account of the People and the Land, in their Social, Sporting, and Mountaineering Aspects. By W. A. BAILLIE GROHMAN. Crown 8vo. with Illustrations, 14s.

Two Years in Fiji, a Descriptive Narrative of a Residence in the Fijian Group of Islands. By LITTON FORBES, M.D. Crown 8vo. 8s. 6d.

Memorials of the Dis- covery and Early Settlement of the Bermudas or Somers Islands, from 1615 to 1685. By Major-General J. H. LEFROY, R.A. C.B. F.R.S. &c. Governor of the Bermudas. 8vo. with Map. [*In the press.*

Eight Years in Ceylon. By Sir SAMUEL W. BAKER, M.A. Crown 8vo. Woodcuts, 7s. 6d.

The Rifle and the Hound in Ceylon. By Sir SAMUEL W. BAKER, M.A. Crown 8vo. Woodcuts, 7s. 6d.

The Dolomite Mountains. Excursions through Tyrol, Carinthia, Carniola, and Friuli. By J. GILBERT and G. C. CHURCHILL, F.R.G.S. Square crown 8vo. Illustrations, 21*s.*

The Alpine Club Map of the Chain of Mont Blanc, from an actual Survey in 1863-1864. By A. ADAMS-REILLY, F.R.G.S. In Chromolithography, on extra stout drawing paper 10*s.* or mounted on canvas in a folding case 12*s.* 6*d.*

The Alpine Club Map of the Valpelline, the Val Tournanche, and the Southern Valleys of the Chain of Monte Rosa, from actual Survey. By A. ADAMS-REILLY, F.R.G.S. Price 6*s.* on extra stout drawing paper, or 7*s.* 6*d.* mounted in a folding case.

Untrodden Peaks and Unfrequented Valleys; a Midsummer Ramble among the Dolomites. By AMELIA B. EDWARDS. With numerous Illustrations. 8vo. 21*s.*

Guide to the Pyrenees, for the use of Mountaineers. By CHARLES PACKE. Crown 8vo. 7*s.* 6*d.*

The Alpine Club Map of Switzerland, with parts of the Neighbouring Countries, on the scale of Four Miles to an Inch. Edited by R. C. NICHOLS, F.R.G.S. In Four Sheets in Portfolio, price 42*s.* coloured, or 34*s.* uncoloured.

The Alpine Guide. By JOHN BALL, M.R.I.A. late President of the Alpine Club. Post 8vo. with Maps and other Illustrations.

The Eastern Alps, 10*s.* 6*d.*

Central Alps, including all the Oberland District, 7*s.* 6*d.*

Western Alps, including Mont Blanc, Monte Rosa, Zermatt, &c. Price 6*s.* 6*d.*

Introduction on Alpine Travelling in general, and on the Geology of the Alps. Price 1*s.* Either of the Three Volumes or Parts of the 'Alpine Guide' may be had with this Introduction prefixed, 1*s.* extra. The 'Alpine Guide' may also be had in Ten separate Parts, or districts, price 2*s.* 6*d.* each.

How to see Norway. By J. R. CAMPBELL. Fcp. 8vo. Map & Woodcuts, 5*s.*

WORKS of FICTION.

The Atelier du Lys; or an Art-Student in the Reign of Terror. By the author of 'Mademoiselle Mori.' Third Edition. Crown 8vo. 6*s.*

Novels and Tales. By the Right Hon. the EARL of BEACONSFIELD. Cabinet Editions, complete in Ten Volumes, crown 8vo. 6*s.* each.

Lothair, 6*s.*	Venetia, 6*s.*
Coningsby, 6*s.*	Alroy, Ixion, &c. 6*s.*
Sybil, 6*s.*	Young Duke &c. 6*s.*
Tancred, 6*s.*	Vivian Grey, 6*s.*
Henrietta Temple, 6*s.*	
Contarini Fleming, &c. 6*s.*	

Whispers from Fairyland. By the Right Hon. E. H. KNATCHBULL-HUGESSEN, M.P. With 9 Illustrations. Crown 8vo. 6*s.*

Higgledy-Piggledy; or, Stories for Everybody and Everybody's Children. By the Right Hon. E. H. KNATCHBULL-HUGESSEN, M.P. With 9 Illustrations. Crown 8vo. 6*s.*

Becker's Gallus; or Roman Scenes of the Time of Augustus. Post 8vo. 7*s.* 6*d.*

Becker's Charicles: Illustrative of Private Life of the Ancient Greeks. Post 8vo. 7*s.* 6*d.*

The Modern Novelist's Library.

Lothair. By the Rt. Hon. the Earl of Beaconsfield. Price 2s. boards; or 2s. 6d. cloth.
Atherstone Priory, 2s. boards; 2s. 6d. cloth.
Mlle. Mori, 2s. boards; 2s. 6d. cloth.
The Burgomaster's Family, 2s. & 2s. 6d.
Malville's Digby Grand, 2s. and 2s. 6d.
———— General Bounce, 2s. & 2s. 6d.
———— Gladiators, 2s. and 2s. 6d.
———— Good for Nothing, 2s. & 2s. 6d.
———— Holmby House, 2s. & 2s. 6d.
———— Interpreter, 2s. and 2s. 6d.
———— Kate Coventry, 2s. and 2s. 6d.
———— Queen's Maries, 2s. & 2s. 6d.
Trollope's Warden, 1s. and 2s. 6d.
———— Barchester Towers, 2s. & 2s. 6d.
Bramley-Moore's Six Sisters of the Valleys, 2s. boards; 2s. 6d. cloth.
Elsa, a Tale of the Tyrolean Alps. Price 2s. boards; 2s. 6d. cloth.
Unawares, a Story of an old French Town. Price 2s. boards; 2s. 6d. cloth.

Stories and Tales. By Elizabeth M. Sewell. Cabinet Edition, in Ten Volumes, each containing a complete Tale or Story —

Amy Herbert, 2s. 6d.
Gertrude, 2s. 6d.
The Earl's Daughter, 2s. 6d.
Experience of Life, 2s. 6d.
Cleve Hall, 2s. 6d.
Ivors, 2s. 6d.
Katharine Ashton, 2s. 6d.
Margaret Percival, 3s. 6d.
Laneton Parsonage, 3s. 6d.
Ursula, 3s. 6d.

Tales of Ancient Greece.
By the Rev. G. W. Cox, M.A. late Scholar of Trinity College, Oxford. Crown 8vo. 6s. 6d.

POETRY and THE DRAMA.

Milton's Lycidas. Edited,
with Notes and Introduction, by C. S. Jerram, M.A. Crown 8vo. 2s. 6d.

Lays of Ancient Rome;
with Ivry and the Armada. By Lord Macaulay. 16mo. 3s. 6d.

Lord Macaulay's Lays of
Ancient Rome. With 90 Illustrations on Wood from Drawings by G. Scharf. Fcp. 4to. 21s.

Miniature Edition of Lord
Macaulay's Lays of Ancient Rome, with G. Scharf's 90 Illustrations reduced in Lithography. Imp. 16mo. 10s. 6d.

Horatii Opera. Library
Edition, with English Notes, Marginal References & various Readings. Edited by the Rev. J. E. Yonge, M.A. 8vo. price 21s.

Southey's Poetical
Works, with the Author's last Corrections and Additions. Medium 8vo. with Portrait, 14s.

Beowulf, a Heroic Poem
of the Eighth Century (Anglo-Saxon Text and English Translation), with Introduction, Notes, and Appendix. By Thomas Arnold, M.A. 8vo. 12s.

Poems by Jean Ingelow.
2 vols. fcp. 8vo. 10s.

First Series, containing 'Divided,' 'The Star's Monument,' &c. Fcp. 8vo. 5s.
Second Series, 'A Story of Doom,' 'Gladys and her Island,' &c. 5s.

Poems by Jean Ingelow.
First Series, with nearly 100 Woodcut Illustrations. Fcp. 4to. 21s.

The Iliad of Homer, Ho-
mometrically translated by C. B. Cayley, Translator of Dante's Comedy, &c. 8vo. 12s. 6d.

The Æneid of Virgil.
Translated into English Verse. By J. Conington, M.A. Crown 8vo. 9s.

Bowdler's Family Shak-
speare. Cheaper Genuine Edition, complete in 1 vol. medium 8vo. large type, with 36 Woodcut Illustrations, 14s. or in 6 vols. fcp. 8vo. 21s.

RURAL SPORTS, HORSE and CATTLE MANAGEMENT, &c.

Annals of the Road; or, Notes on Mail and Stage-Coaching in Great Britain. By Captain MALET. 18th Hussars. To which are added Essays on the Road, by NIMROD. With 3 Woodcuts and 10 Coloured Illustrations. Medium 8vo. 21s.

Down the Road; or, Reminiscences of a Gentleman Coachman. By C. T. S. BIRCH REYNARDSON. Second Edition, with 12 Coloured Illustrations. Medium 8vo. 21s.

Blaine's Encyclopædia of Rural Sports; Complete Accounts, Historical, Practical, and Descriptive, of Hunting, Shooting, Fishing, Racing, &c. With above 600 Woodcuts (20 from Designs by J. LEECH). 8vo. 21s.

A Book on Angling; or, Treatise on the Art of Fishing in every branch; including full Illustrated Lists of Salmon Flies. By FRANCIS FRANCIS. Post 8vo. Portrait and Plates, 15s.

Wilcocks's Sea-Fishermen: comprising the Chief Methods of Hook and Line Fishing, a glance at Nets, and remarks on Boats and Boating. Post 8vo. Woodcuts, 12s. 6d.

The Fly-Fisher's Entomology. By ALFRED RONALDS. With 20 Coloured Plates. 8vo. 14s.

Horses and Stables. By Colonel F. FITZWYGRAM, XV. the King's Hussars. With 24 Plates of Illustrations. 8vo. 10s. 6d.

Youatt on the Horse. Revised and enlarged by W. WATSON, M.R.C.V.S. 8vo. Woodcuts, 12s. 6d.

Youatt's Work on the Dog. Revised and enlarged. 8vo. Woodcuts, 6s.

The Dog in Health and Disease. By STONEHENGE. With 73 Wood Engravings. Square crown 8vo. 7s. 6d.

The Greyhound. By STONEHENGE. Revised Edition, with 25 Portraits of Greyhounds, &c. Square crown 8vo. 15s.

Stables and Stable Fittings. By W. MILES. Imp. 8vo. with 13 Plates, 15s.

The Horse's Foot, and How to keep it Sound. By W. MILES. Imp. 8vo. Woodcuts, 12s. 6d.

A Plain Treatise on Horse-shoeing. By W. MILES. Post 8vo. Woodcuts, 2s. 6d.

Remarks on Horses' Teeth, addressed to Purchasers. By W. MILES. Post 8vo. 1s. 6d.

The Ox, his Diseases and their Treatment; with an Essay on Parturition in the Cow. By J. R. DOBSON, M.R.C.V.S. Crown 8vo. Illustrations, 7s. 6d.

WORKS of UTILITY and GENERAL INFORMATION.

Maunder's Treasury of Knowledge and Library of Reference; comprising an English Dictionary and Grammar, Universal Gazetteer, Classical Dictionary, Chronology, Law Dictionary, Synopsis of the Peerage, Useful Tables, &c. Fcp. 8vo. 6s.

Maunder's Biographical Treasury. Latest Edition, reconstructed and partly re-written, with above 1,600 additional Memoirs, by W. L. R. CATES. Fcp. 8vo. 6s.

Maunder's Scientific and Literary Treasury; a Popular Encyclopædia of Science, Literature, and Art. Latest Edition, in part re-written, with above 1,000 new articles, by J. Y. JOHNSON. Fcp. 8vo. 6s.

Maunder's Treasury of Geography, Physical, Historical, Descriptive, and Political. Edited by W. HUGHES, F.R.G.S. With 7 Maps and 16 Plates. Fcp. 8vo. 6s.

Maunder's Historical Treasury; General Introductory Outlines of Universal History, and a Series of Separate Histories. Revised by the Rev. G. W. COX, M.A. Fcp. 8vo. 6s.

Maunder's Treasury of Natural History; or, Popular Dictionary of Zoology. Revised and corrected Edition. Fcp. 8vo. with 900 Woodcuts, 6s.

The Treasury of Bible Knowledge; being a Dictionary of the Books, Persons, Places, Events, and other Matters of which mention is made in Holy Scripture. By the Rev. J. AYRE, M.A. With Maps, Plates, and many Woodcuts. Fcp. 8vo. 6s.

A Practical Treatise on Brewing; with Formulæ for Public Brewers & Instructions for Private Families. By W. BLACK. 8vo. 10s. 6d.

Chess Openings. By F.W. LONGMAN, Balliol College, Oxford. Second Edition. Fcp. 8vo. 2s. 6d.

English Chess Problems. Edited by J. PIERCE, M.A. and W. T. PIERCE. With 608 Diagrams. Crown 8vo. 12s. 6d.

The Theory of the Modern Scientific Game of Whist. By W. POLE, F.R.S. Eighth Edition. Fcp. 8vo. 2s. 6d.

The Correct Card; or, How to Play at Whist; a Whist Catechism. By Captain A. CAMPBELL-WALKER, F.R.G.S. New Edition. Fcp. 8vo. 2s. 6d.

The Cabinet Lawyer; a Popular Digest of the Laws of England, Civil, Criminal, and Constitutional. Twenty-Fourth Edition, corrected and extended. Fcp. 8vo. 9s.

Pewtner's Comprehensive Specifier; a Guide to the Practical Specification of every kind of Building-Artificer's Work. Edited by W. YOUNG. Crown 8vo. 6s.

Hints to Mothers on the Management of their Health during the Period of Pregnancy and in the Lying-in Room. By THOMAS BULL, M.D. Fcp. 8vo. 2s. 6d.

The Maternal Management of Children in Health and Disease. By THOMAS BULL, M.D. Fcp. 8vo. 2s. 6d.

The Treasury of Botany, or Popular Dictionary of the Vegetable Kingdom; with which is incorporated a Glossary of Botanical Terms. Edited by J. LINDLEY, F.R.S. and T. MOORE, F.L.S. With 274 Woodcuts and 20 Steel Plates. Two Parts, fcp. 8vo. 12s.

D

Modern Cookery for Private Families, reduced to a System of Easy Practice in a Series of carefully-tested Receipts. By ELIZA ACTON. With 8 Plates and 150 Woodcuts. ⬛p. 8vo. 6s.

The Elements of Banking. By H. D. MACLEOD, M.A. Second Edition. Crown 8vo. 7s. 6d.

The Theory and Practice of Banking. By H. D. MACLEOD, M.A. 2 vols. 8vo. 26s.

Our New Judicial System and Civil Procedure as Reconstructed under the Judicature Acts, including the Act of 1876; with Comments on their Effect and Operation. By W. F. FINLASON, Barrister-at-Law. Crown 8vo. 10s. 6d.

Willich's Popular Tables for ascertaining, according to the Carlisle Table of Mortality, the value of Lifehold, Leasehold, and Church Property, Renewal Fines, Reversions, &c. Also Interest, Legacy, Succession Duty, and various other useful tables. Eighth Edition. Post 8vo. 10s.

INDEX.

	PAGE
Acton's Modern Cookery	24
Alpine Club Map of Switzerland	20
Alpine Guide (The)	20
Amos' Jurisprudence	6
—— Primer of the Constitution	6
Anderson's Strength of Materials	16
Armstrong's Childhood of the English Nation	4
Armstrong's Organic Chemistry	12
Arnold's (Dr.) Christian Life	17
—— Lectures on Modern History	3
—— Miscellaneous Works	7
—— School Sermons	17
—— Sermons	17
—— (T.) Manual of English Literature	7
—— Beowulf	21
Arnott's Elements of Physics	11
Atelier (The) du Lys	20
Atherstone Priory	21
Autumn Holidays of a Country Parson	8
Ayre's Treasury of Bible Knowledge	9, 23
Bacon's Essays, by Whately	6
—— Life and Letters, by Spedding	6
—— Works	6
Bain's Mental and Moral Science	7
—— on the Senses and Intellect	7
—— Emotions and Will	7
Baker's Two Works on Ceylon	19
Ball's Guide to the Central Alps	20
—— Guide to the Western Alps	20
—— Guide to the Eastern Alps	20
Bancroft's Native Races of the Pacific	3
Barry on Railway Appliances	16
Beaconsfield's (Lord) Novels and Tales	20
Becker's Charicles and Gallus	20
Bonely's Gracchi, Marius, and Sulla	4
Black's Treatise on Brewing	23
Blackley's German-English Dictionary	9
Blaine's Rural Sports	22
Bloxam's Metals	12
Bolland and Lang's Aristotle's Politics	6
Bowlker on 39 Articles	16
Bourne's Catechism of the Steam Engine	16
—— Handbook of Steam Engine	16
—— Treatise on the Steam Engine	15
—— Improvements in the same	15
Bowdler's Family Shakespeare	21
Bramley-Moore's Six Sisters of the Valleys	21
Brande's Dictionary of Science, Literature, and Art	13
Brinkley's Astronomy	10
Browne's Exposition of the 39 Articles	16

	PAGE
Buckle's History of Civilisation	3
—— Posthumous Remains	7
Bucton's Health in the House	14
Bull's Hints to Mothers	23
—— Maternal Management of Children	23
Burgomaster's Family (The)	21
Burke's Vicissitudes of Families	5
Cabinet Lawyer	23
Campbell's Norway	20
Capes' Age of the Antonines	4
—— Early Roman Empire	4
Cates' Biographical Dictionary	5
—— and Woodward's Encyclopædia	5
Cayley's Iliad of Homer	21
Changed Aspects of Unchanged Truths	8
Chesney's Indian Polity	2
—— Modern Military Biography	2
—— Waterloo Campaign	2
Church's Sketches of Ottoman History	3
Colenso on Moabite Stone &c.	19
—— 's Pentateuch and Book of Joshua	19
Commonplace Philosopher in Town and Country	8
Comte's Positive Polity	5
Congreve's Politics of Aristotle	6
Conington's Translation of Virgil's Æneid	21
—— Miscellaneous Writings	8
Contanseau's Two French Dictionaries	8
Conybeare and Howson's Life and Epistles of St. Paul	17
Counsel and Comfort from a City Pulpit	8
Cox's (G. W.) Aryan Mythology	4
—— Athenian Empire	4
—— Crusades	4
—— General History of Greece	3
—— Greeks and Persians	4
—— History of Greece	3
—— Tales of Ancient Greece	21
Creighton's Age of Elizabeth	3
Cresy's Encyclopædia of Civil Engineering	15
Critical Essays of a Country Parson	8
Crookes's Anthracen	15
—— Chemical Analysis	14
—— Dyeing and Calico-printing	16
Culley's Handbook of Telegraphy	15
Curteis's Macedonian Empire	4
Davidson's Introduction to the New Testament	18
D'Aubigné's Reformation	18
De Caisne and Le Maout's Botany	14

NEW WORKS published by LONGMANS & CO.

	PAGE		PAGE
De Tocqueville's Democracy in America...	5	*Hale's* Fall of the Stuarts....................	4
Dobson on the Ox	22	*Hartley* on the Air	10
Dove's Law of Storms	10	*Hartwig's* Aerial World	12
Dowell's History of Taxes	6	———— Polar World	12
Doyle's (R.) Fairyland	14	———— Sea and its Living Wonders ...	12
		———— Subterranean World...............	13
		———— Tropical World	12
Eastlake's Hints on Household Taste......	15	*Haughton's* Animal Mechanics	11
Edwards's Rambles among the Dolomites	20	*Hayward's* Biographical and Critical Essays	5
———— Nile..	19	*Heer's* Primeval World of Switzerland......	13
———— Year in Western France	19	*Heine's* Life and Works, by Stigand	4
Elements of Botany..............................	13	*Helmholtz* on Tone	11
Ellicott's Commentary on Ephesians	17	*Helmholtz's* Scientific Lectures	11
———— Galatians	17	*Hemsley's* Trees and Shrubs	14
———— Pastoral Epist.	17	*Herschel's* Outlines of Astronomy	10
———— Philippians, &c.	17	*Hinchliff's* Over the Sea and Far Away ...	19
———— Thessalonians .	17	*Hobson's* Amateur Mechanic	15
———— Lectures on Life of Christ	17	*Hoskold's* Engineer's Valuing Assistant ...	15
Elsa, a Tale of the Tyrolean Alps	21	*Howorth's* Mongols.............................	3
Epochs of Ancient History.....................	4	*Hullah's* History of Modern Music	13
———— Modern History	4	———— Transition Period	13
Evans' (J.) Ancient Stone Implements ...	13	*Hume's* Essays	7
———— (A. J.) Bosnia	19	———— Treatise on Human Nature.........	7
Ewald's History of Israel	18		
———— Antiquities of Israel..................	18		
		Ihne's Rome to its Capture.....................	4
		———— History of Rome	3
Fairbairn's Application of Cast and Wrought Iron to Building...	16	Indian Alps	19
———— Information for Engineers......	16	*Ingelow's* Poems	21
———— Life	4		
———— Treatise on Mills and Millwork	16		
Farrar's Chapters on Language	8	*Jameson's* Legends of the Saints & Martyrs	15
———— Families of Speech	8	———— Legends of the Madonna...........	15
Finlason's Judicial System	24	———— Legends of the Monastic Orders	15
Fitzwygram on Horses and Stables.........	22	———— Legends of the Saviour............	15
Forbes's Two Years in Fiji..................	19	*Jenkin's* Electricity and Magnetism.........	12
Frampton's (Bishop) Life	5	*Jerram's* Lycidas of Milton	21
Francis's Fishing Book	22	*Jerrold's* Life of Napoleon	2
Freshfield's Italian Alps	19	*Johnston's* Geographical Dictionary.........	9
Froude's English in Ireland	2	*Jukes's* Types of Genesis	18
———— History of England	2	———— on Second Death	18
———— Short Studies............................	7		
		Kalisch's Commentary on the Bible	17
Gairdner's Houses of Lancaster and York	4	*Keith's* Evidence of Prophecy	17
Ganot's Elementary Physics	11	*Kerl's* Metallurgy, by *Crookes* and *Röhrig*.	16
———— Natural Philosophy	11	*Kirby* and *Spence's* Entomology	12
Gardiner's Buckingham and Charles	2	*Kirkman's* Philosophy	7
———— Personal Government of Charles I.	2	*Knatchbull-Hugessen's* Whispers from Fairy-Land ...	20
———— First Two Stuarts	4	———— Higgledy-Piggledy	20
———— Thirty Years' War	4	*Kuenen's* Prophets and Prophecy in Israel	17
Geffcken's Church and State	6		
German Home Life..............................	7		
Gilbert & Churchill's Dolomites	20		
Girdlestone's Bible Synonyms.................	17		
Goldziher's Hebrew Mythology...............	17	Landscapes, Churches, &c.......................	8
Goodeve's Mechanics	12	*Latham's* English Dictionaries	8
———— Mechanism............................	12	———— Handbook of English Language	8
Grant's Ethics of Aristotle	6	*Lawrence* on Rocks	13
Graver Thoughts of a Country Parson......	8	*Lecky's* History of European Morals.........	3
Greville's Journal	2	———— Rationalism	3
Griffin's Algebra and Trigonometry.........	12	———— Leaders of Public Opinion.........	5
Griffith's Behind the Veil.....................	18	*Lefroy's* Bermudas	19
Grohman's Tyrol and the Tyrolese	19	Leisure Hours in Town	8
Grove (Sir W. R.) on Correlation of Physical Forces.........	11	Lessons of Middle Age	8
———— (F. C.) The Frosty Caucasus	19	*Lewes's* Biographical History of Philosophy	4
Gwilt's Encyclopædia of Architecture......	15	*Lewis* on Authority	7

Liddell and *Scott's* Greek-English Lexicon ... 9
Lindley and *Moore's* Treasury of Botany .. 13. 20
Lloyd's Magnetism 11
——— Wave-Theory of Light 11
Longman's (F. W.) Chess Openings........... 29
——————— German Dictionary ... 9
——————— (W.) Edward the Third 2
——————— Lectures on History of England 2
——————— Old and New St. Paul's 15
London's Encyclopædia of Agriculture ... 16
——————— Gardening 16
——————— Plants 15
Lubbock's Origin of Civilisation 13
Ludlow's American War............................... 4
Lyra Germanica 18

Macaulay's (Lord) Essays 1
——————— History of England ... 1
——————— Lays of Ancient Rome 14, 21
——————— Life and Letters 4
——————— Miscellaneous Writings 7
——————— Speeches 7
——————— Works 1
——————— Writings, Selections from 7
MacColl's Eastern Question 1
McCulloch's Dictionary of Commerce 9
Macleod's Economical Philosophy 6
——— Theory and Practice of Banking 24
——— Elements of Banking............... 24
Mademoiselle Mori 21
Malet's Annals of the Road 20
Marshall's Physiology 14
Marshman's Life of Havelock 5
Martineau's Christian Life 19
——————— Hours of Thought............ 19
——————— Hymns 18
Maunder's Biographical Treasury 5. 23
——————— Geographical Treasury 23
——————— Historical Treasury 23
——————— Scientific and Literary Treasury 23
——————— Treasury of Knowledge........9. 23
——————— Treasury of Natural History..13. 23
Maxwell's Theory of Heat 10
May's History of Democracy...................... 2
——— History of England 2
Melville's Digby Grand 21
——————— General Bounce 21
——————— Gladiators 21
——————— Good for Nothing 21
——————— Holmby House 21
——————— Interpreter 21
——————— Kate Coventry 21
——————— Queen's Maries 21
Mendelssohn's Letters 4
Merivale's Fall of the Roman Republic ... 3
——————— General History of Rome 3
——————— Roman Triumvirates............ 4
——————— Romans under the Empire ... 3
Merrifield's Arithmetic and Mensuration... 12
Miles on Horse's Foot and Horse Shoeing 20
——— on Horse's Teeth and Stables......... 20
Mill (J.) on the Mind 6
——— Dissertations & Discussions............. 6
——— Essays on Religion 17
——— Hamilton's Philosophy 6
——— (J. S.) Liberty 5
——— Political Economy 5

Mill (J. S.) Representative Government ... 5
——————— System of Logic 6
——————— Unsettled Questions 5
——————— Utilitarianism 5
——————— Autobiography 5
Miller's Elements of Chemistry 14
——————— Inorganic Chemistry............ 12
Mitchell's Manual of Assaying 26
Modern Novelist's Library 21
Monsell's Spiritual Songs 18
Moore's Irish Melodies, Illustrated Edition 15
——————— Lalla Rookh, Illustrated Edition 15
Morell's Mental Philosophy 7
Mozart's Life and Letters 4
Müller's Chips from a German Workshop 8
——————— Science of Language 8
——————— Science of Religion 8

Nelson on the Moon 10
New Testament, Illustrated Edition........... 15
Nevill's Puzzle of Life 18
Northcott's Lathes & Turning 26

O'Conor's Commentary on Hebrews 18
——————— Romans 18
——————— St. John 18
Osborn's Islam 3
Owen's Comparative Anatomy and Physiology of Vertebrate Animals 14

Packe's Guide to the Pyrenees 20
Pattison's Casaubon 5
Payen's Industrial Chemistry.................... 15
Preston's Comprehensive Specifier 23
Pierce's Chess Problems 23
Pole's Game of Whist 23
Prescott & *Sivewright's* Telegraphy........... 10
Present-Day Thoughts 8
Proctor's Astronomical Essays 10
——————— Moon 10
——————— Orbs around Us 10
——————— Other Worlds than Ours ... 10
——————— Saturn 10
——————— Scientific Essays (Two Series) ... 10
——————— Sun 10
——————— Transits of Venus 10
——————— Two Star Atlases................ 10
——————— Universe 10
Prothero's De Montfort 2
Public Schools Atlas of Ancient Geography 9
——————— Atlas of Modern Geography 9

Rawlinson's Parthia................................... 3
——————— Sassanians..................... 3
Recreations of a Country Parson 8
Redgrave's Dictionary of Artists 14
Rave's Residence in Vienna and Berlin ... 19
Reilly's Map of Mont Blanc 20
——————— Monte Rosa 20
Rowsby's Memoirs 5
Reynardson's Down the Road 20

	PAGE
Rich's Dictionary of Antiquities	9
Rivers's Rose Amateur's Guide	13
Rogers's Eclipse of Faith	17
——— Defence of Eclipse of Faith	17
——— Essays	5
Roget's Thesaurus of English Words and Phrases	8
Ronald's Fly-Fisher's Entomology	22
Roscoe's Outlines of Civil Procedure	6
Rothschild's Israelites	18
Sandars's Justinian's Institutes	6
Sankey's Sparta and Thebes	4
Savile on Apparitions	8
——— on Primitive Faith	17
Schellen's Spectrum Analysis	10
Scott's Lectures on the Fine Arts	14
——— Poems	14
Seaside Musing	8
Seebohm's Oxford Reformers of 1498	3
——— Protestant Revolution	4
Sewell's History of France	2
——— Passing Thoughts on Religion	18
——— Preparation for Communion	18
——— Questions of the Day	18
——— Self-Examination for Confirmation	18
——— Stories and Tales	21
——— Thoughts for the Age	18
Shelley's Workshop Appliances	12
Short's Church History	3
Smith's (Sydney) Essays	7
——— Wit and Wisdom	7
——— (Dr. R. A.) Air and Rain	10
——— (R. B.) Rome and Carthage	4
Southey's Poetical Works	21
Stanley's History of British Birds	13
Stephen's Ecclesiastical Biography	5
Stonehenge on the Dog	22
——— on the Greyhound	22
Stoney on Strains	16
Stubbs's Early Plantagenets	4
Sunday Afternoons at the Parish Church of a University City	8
Supernatural Religion	18
Swinbourne's Picture Logic	6
Taylor's History of India	2
——— Manual of Ancient History	4
——— Manual of Modern History	4
——— *(Jeremy)* Works, edited by *Eden*	18
Text-Books of Science	12
Thomé's Structural and Physiological Botany	12, 13
Thomson's Laws of Thought	7
Thorpe's Quantitative Analysis	12
Thorpe and *Muir's* Qualitative Analysis	12
Tilden's Chemical Philosophy	12, 14

	PAGE
Todd on Parliamentary Government	2
Trench's Realities of Irish Life	7
Trollope's Barchester Towers	21
——— Warden	21
Twiss's Law of Nations	6
Tyndall's American Lectures on Light	11
——— Diamagnetism	11
——— Fragments of Science	11
——— Heat a Mode of Motion	11
——— Lectures on Electricity	11
——— Lectures on Light	11
——— Lectures on Sound	11
——— Molecular Physics	11
Unawares	21
Unwin's Machine Design	12
Ure's Dictionary of Arts, Manufactures, and Mines	16
Vaughan's Trident, Crescent, and Cross	18
Walker on Whist	23
Warburton's Edward the Third	4
Watson's Geometry	12
Watts's Dictionary of Chemistry	14
Webb's Objects for Common Telescopes	10
Weinhold's Experimental Physics	11
Wellington's Life, by *Gleig*	5
Whately's English Synonymes	8
——— Logic	6
——— Rhetoric	6
White and *Riddle's* Latin Dictionaries	9
Whitworth's Measuring Machine	15
Wilcocks's Sea-Fisherman	22
Williams's Aristotle's Ethics	6
Willich's Popular Tables	24
Wood's (J. G.) Bible Animals	12
——— Homes without Hands	12
——— Insects at Home	12
——— Insects Abroad	12
——— Out of Doors	12
——— Strange Dwellings	12
——— (J. T.) Ephesus	19
Woodward's Geology	13
Wyatt's History of Prussia	2
Yonge's English-Greek Lexicons	9
——— Horace	21
Youatt on the Dog	22
——— on the Horse	22
Zeller's Plato	3
——— Socrates	3
——— Stoics, Epicureans, and Sceptics	3
Zimmern's Life of Schopenhauer	4

MODERN HISTORICAL EPOCHS.

In course of publication, each volume in fcap. 8vo. complete in itself,

EPOCHS OF MODERN HISTORY:

A SERIES OF BOOKS NARRATING THE

HISTORY of ENGLAND and EUROPE

At SUCCESSIVE EPOCHS SUBSEQUENT to the CHRISTIAN ERA.

EDITED BY

E. E. MORRIS, M.A. Lincoln Coll. Oxford;
J. S. PHILLPOTTS, B.C.L. New Coll. Oxford; and
C. COLBECK, M.A. Fellow of Trin. Coll. Oxford.

'This striking collection of little volumes is a valuable contribution to the literature of the day, whether for youthful or more mature readers. As an abridgment of several important phases of modern history it has great merit, and some of its parts display powers and qualities of a high order. Such writers, indeed, as Professor Stubbs, Messrs. Warburton, Gairdner, Creighton, and others, could not fail to give us excellent work. . . . The style of the series is, as a general rule, correct and pure, in the case of Mr. Seebohm it more than once rises into genuine, simple, and manly eloquence; and the composition of some of the volumes displays no ordinary historical skill. . . . The Series is and deserves to be popular.'

THE TIMES, Jan. 2, 1877.

Eleven Volumes Now Published:—

The ERA of the PROTESTANT REVOLUTION. By F. SEEBOHM, Author of 'The Oxford Reformers—Colet, Erasmus, More.' With 4 Coloured Maps and 12 Diagrams on Wood. Price 2s. 6d.

'Mr. Seebohm's Era of the Protestant Revolution shows an admirable mastery of a complex subject; it abounds in sound and philosophic thought, and as a composition it is very well ordered. . . . This volume, in short, is of the greatest merit.'
THE TIMES, Jan. 2.

The CRUSADES. By the Rev. G. W. Cox, M.A. late Scholar of Trinity College, Oxford; Author of the 'Aryan Mythology' &c. With a Coloured Map. Price 2s. 6d.

'The earliest period, in point of time, is that of the Crusades, of which we have a summary from the accomplished pen of the well-known Author of one of the best and latest histories of Greece. Mr. Cox's narrative is flowing and easy, and parts of his work are extremely good.'
THE TIMES, Jan. 2.

The THIRTY YEARS' WAR, 1618–1648. By SAMUEL RAWSON GARDINER, late Student of Ch. Ch.; Author of 'History of England from the Accession of James I. to the Disgrace of Chief Justice Coke' &c. With a Coloured Map. Price 2s. 6d.

'The narrative—a singularly perplexing task—is on the whole remarkably clear, and the Author gives us a well-written summary of the causes that led to the great contest, and of the most striking incidents that marked its progress. Mr. Gardiner's judgments, too, are usually just. . . . The Author, we should add, is very skilful in his delineation of historical characters.'
THE TIMES, Jan. 2.

The HOUSES of LANCASTER and YORK; with the CONQUEST and LOSS of FRANCE. By JAMES GAIRDNER, of the Public Record Office; Editor of 'The Paston Letters' &c. With 5 Coloured Maps. Price 2s. 6d.

'Mr. Gairdner's Epoch, 'Lancaster and York, is usually correct and sensible, and the conclusions of the Author are just and accurate.'
THE TIMES, Jan. 2.

London, LONGMANS & CO. [*Continued.*

EPOCHS OF MODERN HISTORY—continued.

EDWARD THE THIRD. By the Rev. W. WARBURTON, M.A. late Fellow of All Souls College, Oxford; Her Majesty's Senior Inspector of Schools. With 3 Coloured Maps and 3 Genealogical Tables. Price 2s. 6d.

'This Epoch is a very good one, and is well worth a studious reader's attention. Mr. WARBURTON has reproduced extremely well the spirit and genius of that chivalric age.' THE TIMES, Jan. 2.

The AGE of ELIZABETH. By the Rev. M. CREIGHTON, M.A. late Fellow and Tutor of Merton College, Oxford. With 5 Maps and 4 Genealogical Tables. 2s. 6d.

'Mr. CREIGHTON has thoroughly mastered the intricate mysteries of the foreign politics of the whole period; and he has described extremely ably the relations between this country and the other States of Europe, and the character of the policy of the Queen and her counsellors.' THE TIMES, Jan. 2.

The FALL of the STUARTS; and WESTERN EUROPE from 1678 to 1697. By the Rev. EDWARD HALE, M.A. Assistant-Master at Eton. With Eleven Maps and Plans. Price 2s. 6d.

'Mr. HALE has thoroughly grasped the great facts of the time, and has placed them in a very effective light.' THE TIMES, Jan. 2.

The FIRST TWO STUARTS and the PURITAN REVOLUTION, 1603-1660. By SAMUEL RAWSON GARDINER, Author of 'The Thirty Years' War, 1618-1648.' With 4 Coloured Maps. Price 2s. 6d.

'Mr. GARDINER'S "First Two Stuarts and the Puritan Revolution" deserves more notice than we can bestow upon it. This is in some respects a very striking work. Mr. GARDINER'S sketch of the time of James I. brings out much that had hitherto been little known.' THE TIMES, Jan. 2.

The WAR of AMERICAN INDEPENDENCE, 1775-1783. By JOHN MALCOLM LUDLOW, Barrister-at-Law. With 4 Coloured Maps. Price 2s. 6d.

'Mr. LUDLOW'S account of the obscure annals of what afterwards became the Thirteen Colonies is learned, judicious, and full of interest, and his description of the Red Indian communities is admirable for its good feeling and insight. . . . The volume is characterised by impartiality and good sense.' THE TIMES, Jan. 2.

The EARLY PLANTAGENETS. By the Rev. W. STUBBS, M.A. Regius Professor of Modern History in the University of Oxford. With 2 coloured Maps. Price 2s. 6d.

'As a whole, his book is one of rare excellence. As a comprehensive sketch of the period it is worthy of very high commendation. . . . As an analyst of institutions and laws Mr. STUBBS is certainly not inferior to HALLAM. His narrative, moreover, is, as a rule, excellent, clear, well put together, and often picturesque; his language is always forcible and sometimes eloquent; his power of condensation is very remarkable, and his chapter on the contemporaneous state of Europe is admirable for its breadth and conciseness.' THE TIMES, Jan. 2.

The AGE of ANNE. By E. E. MORRIS, M.A. of Lincoln College, Oxford; Head Master of the Melbourne Grammar School, Australia; Original Editor of the Series. With 7 Maps and Plans. Price 2s. 6d.

Volumes in preparation, in continuation of the Series :—

The NORMANS in EUROPE. By Rev. A. H. JOHNSON, M.A., Fellow of All Souls College, Oxford. [*Nearly ready.*]

The BEGINNING of the MIDDLE AGES; Charles the Great and Alfred; the History of England in connexion with that of Europe in the Ninth Century. By the Very Rev. R. W. CHURCH, M.A. Dean of St. Paul's. [*In the press.*

The EARLY HANOVERIANS. By the Rev. T. J. LAWRENCE, B.A. Warden of Cavendish College, late Fellow and Tutor of Downing College, Cambridge.

The FRENCH REVOLUTION to the BATTLE of WATERLOO, 1789-1815. By BERTHA M. CORDERY, Author of 'The Struggle Against Absolute Monarchy.'

FREDERICK the GREAT and the SEVEN YEARS' WAR. By F. W. LONGMAN, of Balliol College, Oxford.

London, LONGMANS & CO.

www.ingramcontent.com/pod-product-compliance
Lightning Source LLC
Chambersburg PA
CBHW020312170426
43202CB00008B/580